OCCASI

The Qurʾān *and* The Sunnah

Ismaʿīl Rājī al Fārūqī
Lois Lamyāʾ al Fārūqī

THE INTERNATIONAL INSTITUTE OF ISLAMIC THOUGHT
LONDON · WASHINGTON

P.O. BOX 669, HERNDON, VA 20172, USA
www.iiit.org

LONDON OFFICE
P.O. BOX 126, RICHMOND, SURREY TW9 2UD, UK
www.iiituk.com

978-1-56564-655-1

IMAGES P. 8, 10, 12, 14, 21, 24, 49, 54, 74, *Wikimedia Commons*

Typesetting and Cover design by Shiraz Khan

Series Editors
DR. ANAS S. AL-SHAIKH-ALI
SHIRAZ KHAN

Foreword

THE INTERNATIONAL INSTITUTE OF ISLAMIC THOUGHT (IIIT) has great pleasure in presenting Occasional Paper 25 *The Qur'ān and the Sunnah* by Ismaʿīl al Fārūqī and Lois Lamyā' al Fārūqī.

Professor Ismaʿīl Rājī al Fārūqī (1921–1986) was a Palestinian-American philosopher, visionary, and an authority in comparative religion. A great contemporary scholar of Islam, his scholarship encompassed the whole spectrum of Islamic Studies, covering areas such as the study of religion, Islamic thought, approaches to knowledge, history, culture, education, interfaith dialogue, aesthetics, ethics, politics, economics, and science. Without doubt al Fārūqī was one of the great Muslim scholars of the 20th century.

Professor Lois Lamyā' al Fārūqī (Lois Ibsen) (1926–1986), wife of Ismaʿīl Rājī al Fārūqī was an expert in Islamic art and music. She taught at the universities of Butler, Pennsylvania, Villanova and Temple University (USA). Her publications include *An Annotated Glossary of Arabic Musical Terms*, and *Women, Muslim Society, and Islam.*

The IIIT, established in 1981, has served as a major center to facilitate serious scholarly efforts based on Islamic vision, values and principles. The Institute's programs of research, seminars and conferences during the last thirty years have resulted in the publication of more than four hundred titles in English and Arabic, many of which have been translated into other major languages.

ANAS S. AL-SHAIKH-ALI
Academic Advisor, IIIT London Office

The Qur'ān

Data Revelata and The History of Prophecy

REVELATION, OR THE COMMUNICATION OF GOD'S WILL TO MAN, has a long history, and has taken various forms. In the earliest times, God, or the being assumed to be divine, revealed his will indirectly through the omens of nature, or directly through visions and dreams, which the priesthood was initiated to decipher and charged to communicate and implement. The *data revelata* were preserved by being committed to memory. They were recalled, recited, or invoked on ceremonial occasions. Some were thus translated into and had become a living tradition; others were forgotten or transformed into something else after the passing of the original recipients of revelation. Naturally, all were subject to forgetfulness, personal interpretation, and the shifting vicissitudes of the needs and conditions of the carriers. Their recording or textualization was late and, at any rate, had to await the invention of writing. The idea that the *verba* of a divine message is holy and hence object of a religious taboo against tampering with it, may be as old as revelation itself. However, the earliest text of a divine message containing a claim of such holiness or taboo – and thus establishing by internal evidence that the promulgators of that message regarded it as such – is the Code of Hammurabi. Its evidence is partly graphic and partly verbal. The former presents Hammurabi in reverential posture before the god of Justice, Shamash, Who hands to him the law. The latter consists in

Hammurabi's own affirmation that the law was committed to him by the god who remains its ultimate executor and keeper, and the code's threat to those who would tamper with its text.[1] In a passage reflecting

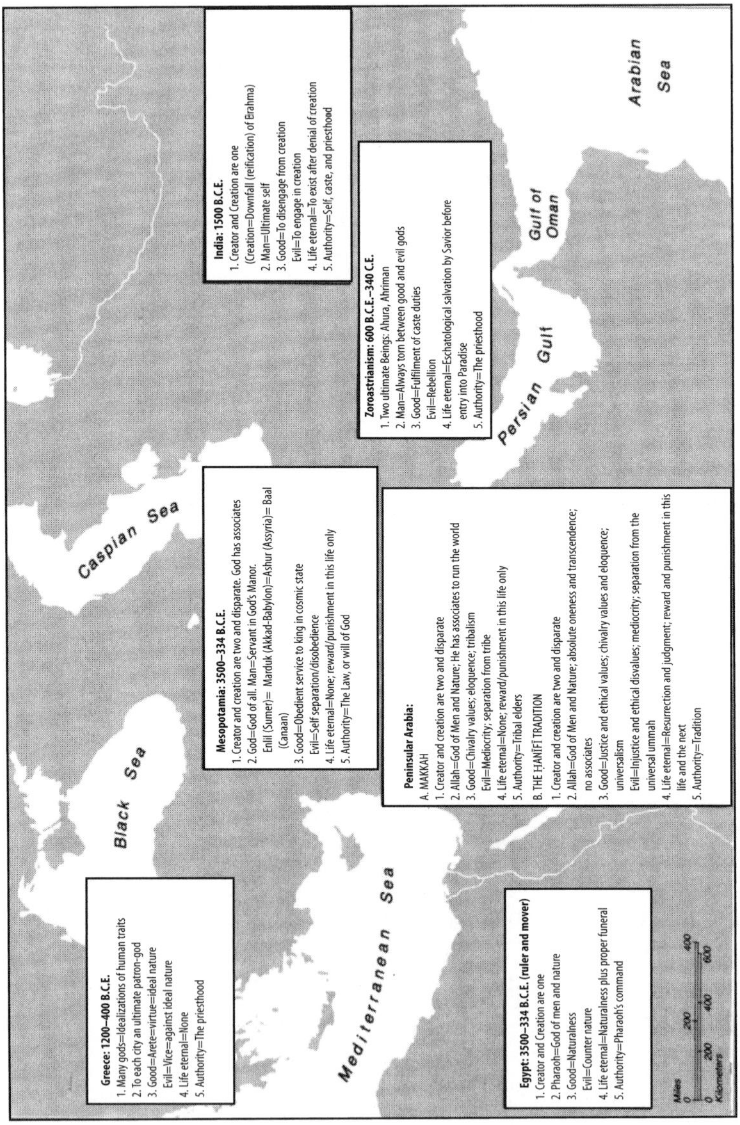

Map 17. Religion in the Ancient Near East.

the Ḥanīfī tradition of Peninsular Arabia, the Qur'ān refers to *ṣuḥuf* (revealed texts) of Ibrahīm (Abraham).[2] Although archeology has not yet uncovered a physical proof of their existence, it is not unreasonable to assume their existence. Since historians have agreed to place Ibrahim in the patriarchal age 2000–1400 B.C. – it is likely that he knew how to read and write, and regarded the text of a divine message as reverently as did Hammurabi's contemporaries who were themselves Ibrahīm's compatriots and fellows.[3]

The next claim of this kind is one made on behalf of King Hezekiah who reigned in Judah from 715 to 687 B.C.E. Hezekiah's claim to fame is the reform he achieved, which sought to centralize the cultic observances of the Hebrews, a reform alleged to fulfill a requirement of a Deuteronomic text and hence implying both the existence of the text and its being held sacred by the people. However, no law book is even hinted at in connection with that reform.[4] A "book" is indeed mentioned in connection with the reform of a later successor to Hezekiah's throne, Josiah (640–609 B.C.E.), and this constitutes the third claim of its kind (II Kings 22:8). Instructed by the king to bring out the hoard of silver from the Temple's vault to spend it on repairing its walls, Hilkiah, the high priest, found a "book of the law" for which he could not vouch.[5] The king ordered his ministers as well as Hilkiah to go out to the people and ask "all Judah concerning the words of anybody regarding this book" unto which "our fathers have not hearkened." None rose to the bait but a certain Huldah, a "prophetess" of doubtful reputation, seized the occasion to defend the anti-Canaanization, anti-assimilation view of the book which neither king nor high priest ever knew (II Kings 22:11–20). Later, a fourth claim presented itself. "The word of God" which came to Jeremiah was thrown into the fire by King Jehoiakim around 598–597 B.C.E. because it threatened dire punishment for Judah at Babylon's hands (Jeremiah 36:20ff). This did not destroy it because Jeremiah could recite it from memory. However, the redactor of the Book of Jeremiah saw fit to warn the reader that to that very word of God that came to Jeremiah, "there were added besides unto them many like words" (Jeremiah 36:32). Two centuries later, a fifth claim was made when Ezra introduced yet another version of the law of God which scholars classify as P in contrast to the earlier versions of J and E, as well as D, the above-mentioned law book of Josiah, Hilkiah, and Huldah.[6] Throughout the two millennia of pre-Christian history, the Hebrews certainly received numerous revelations. But there is no evidence that they ever agreed upon or kept a text in a way worthy of its divine provenance. It was at the Council of Jamnia (Yibna) in 100 C.E. that a body of old inherited texts, redacted and edited numerous times by unknown persons, was declared holy and hence "defiling the hands" that touched them.[7] Even then, the texts known as "Latter Prophets" and "Writings" were not finally fixed but were to suffer addition. Canonization was a long process in which the Pentateuch was first to be recognized as canonical, followed by the other parts of the corpus.

This development in the texts of revelation was in large part determined by changing attitudes toward the phenomenon of prophecy. In Mesopotamia, the king and the provincial governors he appointed acted as receivers of the messages from Heaven, and as conveyors of its contents to the people. Reverence for the divine was thus joined to reverence for the state and its officers. This reverence never waned but continued regardless of the growth or decline of the state and its power. Although the Hebrews issued from the same Mesopotamian background, they seem to have lapsed into more primitive forms during the centuries following their exodus from Ur. Jacob's stealing the gods of his employer-uncle (Genesis 31:19–22), his wrestling with God-as-ghost near the Jordan River (Genesis 32:24–32), and the intermarriage of the Beni Elohim (literally the sons of gods) with the daughters of men (Genesis 6:2–4) – granted the antiquity of the J and E sources – point to the level of Hebrew popular religiosity in Canaan rather than to the lofty one of their ancestors in Mesopotamia.

Through his association with Jethro, High Priest of Midyan, Moses, who grew up as an Egyptian in religion and culture, quickly undid his upbringing and recaptured his Mesopotamian inheritance. He saw God as speaking to him directly in a message containing the essentials of the law, not unlike Hammurabi. However, as the Hebrews and their colleagues, the Amphictyonites who rallied with and accompanied them in their drive toward Canaan, settled there, they returned to the Canaanite practices they had learned before they went to Egypt.

In the period of the Judges and down to David (1200–1000 B.C.E.), whole villages practiced prophecy with trumpet and drum and singing and dancing (II Kings 4:1). The whole populace would plunge into an orgy of "prophesying" (I Samuel 10:5, 10; 19:18). Under Samuel, David, and Solomon, the Old Testament evidence shows, prophecy became tame, and the prophets, now turned almost into priests – Samuel, Jeremiah, Ezekiel, and Pashhur were both (Isaiah 8:2; Jeremiah 20:1–6) – invariably advocated the monarchy and its policies like state functionaries. State functionaries they certainly became under David, who used them to voice the plea that his kingdom was God's and his dynasty was eternal. During Solomon's reign dissatisfaction with his policies expressed itself through some dissenting voices critical of the monarchy. After his death, prophecy disengaged itself from the state and established itself as the authoritative autonomous voice of God. For several centuries the prophets relayed to the people divine pronouncements that were critical and often condemnatory of royalty, state policy and administration, and popular religious and social practices. It was in this period that prophecy attained greater heights than were achieved in Mesopotamia. Jeremiah compared the word of God to a ball of fire that cannot be conjured and that, when it comes, can only be passed on with all its integrity. This apogee did not last. Soon prophecy degenerated with the decay of Israel until nobody could differentiate between the true prophet and the false ones who were circulating among the Hebrews everywhere by the hundreds.

Calligraphy panel from a contemporary mosque in Kuwait. Central Medallion: Basmalah; middle circle: Qur'ān 33:35; outer circle: Qur'ān 91:1-15. [Courtesy ʿIṣām Tājī.]

Jesus came in the midst of this degeneration of the phenomenon of prophecy. Hebrew scripture had already been canonized, and Jesus invoked it on every occasion. Both speaker and audience must have assumed its divine origin and sacredness, its authority and unchangeableness. This notwithstanding, no one of Jesus' disciples, who were all Jews well acquainted with the taboo of a revealed message, revered the new revelation of Jesus enough to commit it to memory or record it.

Obviously, this could not be expected of his detractors and enemies, or generally of the unbelievers. But the strange fact is equally true of his believing followers. A few anecdotes from his life, coupled with a few of the parables he taught, some proverbs and common sayings he quoted along with his recollection of some passages of Hebrew scripture, are all that survived of his message. Nothing of this was kept in the original tongue Jesus spoke, namely Aramaic. All came down filtered through Greek, a tongue alien to Jesus and his audience in its vocabulary as well as its categories of thought. Scholars speak of a "Jewish" or "Palestinian" Christianity battling Hellenic Christianity and the form which the message of Jesus had taken soon after appearance. The latter triumphed and dominated; the "Aramaic message" of Jesus disappeared forever.

These circumstances, unfortunate for the historian of the texts of revelation, moved Ibn Ḥazm, the greatest comparativist before modern times and the first textual critic of the Old and New Testaments, to open his analysis of the New Testament with a feeling of relief. "The Torah," he wrote,

> is claimed by its adherents to be the verbatim word of God conveyed by Him to Moses and written down by his own hand. That is why I had to write the foregoing long assiduous analysis of its text to establish the contrary. Fortunately, no Christian makes this kind of claim regarding the New Testament. All Christians agree that the New Testament text is a composite of works by the four evangelists – Matthew, Mark, Luke, and John – and a number of other writings by humans.[8]

Climax of The Phenomenon of Prophecy

In a sense, Hammurabi, Moses, and Jeremiah represent apogees of the phenomenon of prophecy. Each one of them regarded God as revealing to him His will through words which are absolutely His – verbatim – absolutely commanding, imperative, and carrying a measure of numinousness to make them at once sacred and unalterable. However, were the three messengers to return to earth today, they would not recognize

Mosque, Ottawa, Canada, completed 1981.

what is attributed to them as their own. Perhaps Hammurabi alone might recognize the code bearing his name as his own. The text of the code we have comes from a stela that was carried away from Mesopotamia to Susa by raiding Elamites between 1207 and 1171 B.C.E., more than five centuries after Hammurabi. Whether the stela was a true copy of the original we will never know. Even so, it was disfigured by the Elamites; and the missing parts had to be filled in from still later copies of the code.[9]

Al Rashīd Mosque, Canadian Islamic Centre, Edmonton, Albetra, compeleted 1982.

Moses and Jeremiah, on the other hand, would be hard put to find in the texts of the Old Testament anything that is in language, form, or content truly their own, communicated by them as the message from Heaven. Not only were the texts of their messages heavily altered by countless collectors and editors, but their very language has long been dead and forgotten. Whatever is attributed to them passed through numerous languages, peoples, and ages, each of which conceived it in its own idiom or language, and molded and repatterned it in different modes of feeling and thinking different from those of the messengers themselves or of their first audiences. Even if the Old Testament is to be trusted in its ascriptions, the real messages of these prophets, like those of all divine messengers before them, lie buried under impenetrable and forever insoluble hermeneutical problems – linguistic, idiomatic,

Spiral minaret of Grand Mosque of Al Mutawakkil, Sāmarrā, Iraq.

syntactical, formal (lexicographic, grammatical, redactional, stylistic, ideational), structural, and historical.

We have a completely different case in the message of Muḥammad conveyed in the last two decades before his death in 10/632. Both the Prophethood of Muḥammad and the Qur'ān he conveyed as the message dictated to him by the angel on behalf of God represent the highest and ultimate development of the phenomenon of prophecy. Unlike any prophet before him, were Muḥammad to return today, he would doubtless acknowledge the Qur'ān to be the selfsame text he received from God and conveyed to his companions.

The text has been preserved absolutely intact. Not one jot or tittle has changed. Diacritical marks have been added and the calligraphy has been improved to facilitate its correct reading and recitation. Its parts stand today in exactly the same order in which the Prophet was instructed by the Angel to arrange them. Moreover, the language the Prophet and his contemporaries spoke is still alive. It is read, written, and spoken by the millions. Its grammar, syntax, idioms, literary forms – the media of expression and the constituents of literary beauty – all are still the same as they were in the Prophet's time. All this makes of the Qur'ān a phenomenon of human culture without parallel.

The Qur'ān as Divine *Ipsissima Verba*

The Qur'ān is a text of 114 *suwar* (sing. *sūrah*) or chapters, 6,616 *āyāt* or verses, 77,934 words, and 323,671 letters. It was revealed in Makkah and Madīnah and their environs – hence the characterization of its *suwar* as Makkī or Madanī – several verses at a time. Except for the first few revelations, which took the Prophet Muḥammad completely by surprise, each of the revelations had a situational context to which it spoke. Most of these, if not all, are known to scholars as *asbāb al nuzūl* (the situational causes of revelation). From the first to last, each revelation was first impressed upon the Prophet's memory, who then conveyed the revelations verbatim to his relatives or companions, who memorized and recited them in turn, and finally recorded them in a text. At the end of his life, Muḥammad had about 30,000 contemporaries who had heard and memorized the Qur'ān in whole or in part. Several of them could read and write and had committed the Qur'ān to writing in part or in toto. Certainly, writing materials were crude: leather, bones, stone or wood, cloth, and papyrus.

Map 18. Makkah al Mukarramah at the time of the Prophet.

Since revelation of the Qur'ān was a cumulative process over some twenty-three years, the Prophet arranged and rearranged the revelations year by year. This took place during the month of fasting – Ramaḍān – when the Angel Gabriel would instruct the Prophet where to intercalate and include the new passages, and the Prophet would then recite liturgically and publicly all that had been revealed up till then in the new order given to him by the Angel. For fourteen centuries, following this practice of the Prophet, Muslims by the hundreds of thousands have liturgically and publicly recited the Qur'ān from memory. Under Islamic law, recitation of the Qur'ān in *ṣalāt* – the ritual of worship – may not be interrupted except by loss of ritual purity or death; but it can and should be interrupted in case of error in the recitation. In that case any other worshipper may raise his voice with the correct recitation of the misread, omitted, or mispronounced passage.

The Qur'ān was also committed to writing. Being illiterate, the Prophet engaged a scribe to write down the revelation. Many others

Mosque of Sulaymān the Magnificent, Istanbūl, Turkey.

wrote it down as well. In the year Muḥammad died, all the revelations written by the Prophet's scribe were collected and stored in the house of ʿĀ'ishah, the Prophet's wife and daughter of Abū Bakr, the first khalīfah (caliph). Twelve years later, as many non-Peninsular Arabs and non-Arabic speaking peoples converted to Islam and recited the Qur'ān with some mistakes, the Prophet's scribe was ordered to head a commission of the Prophet's literate companions, of those who were most able in memory, to prepare a written text of the Qur'ān. This was completed within the year, and several copies were made and distributed. One of these old copies is extant and is kept in Bukhārā. Except for the diacritical marks and some improvements of orthography and calligraphy, the Qur'ān extant in every Muslim home around the world today, or kept and recited from memory by the millions, is identical to the material that was recited and conveyed by the Prophet to his companions fourteen centuries ago.

There is no history of the text of the Qur'ān. Nor can there be one other than that which traces the shape and use of diacritical marks and calligraphic forms. Some Orientalists have misunderstood the fact that a few words of the Qur'ān could be read with slightly differing accentuation, or replaced by others of the same length, construction, and, in most cases, meaning. These variants of recitation were authorized by the Prophet himself, and were kept as exegetical footnotes in commentaries, or passed from generation to generation as a *qirā'ah* or "recitation tradition." These variants affect neither the form nor the substance nor meaning of the Qur'ān. They exist at all because they were tolerated by the Prophet, who may have authorized a variant pronunciation because it agreed with the reciter's tribal or local linguistic tradition. Muslims agree that the Qur'ān was revealed in the linguistic tradition of Quraysh, the dominant tribe of Makkah. That is why the Quraysh recitation is basic, and the others are tolerated and included in footnotes and commentaries for use by the interested. None of this warrants the appellation "history."[10] Other Orientalists have investigated the problem and have concluded with William Muir that "we might beyond the strongest presumption affirm that every verse in the Kor'an is the genuine and unaltered composition of Muḥammad himself, and conclude with at least a close approximation to the verdict of von Hammer that we hold the Kor'an to be as surely Muḥammad's word, as the Muḥammadans hold it to be the word of God." [11] Thus, accordance between the judgment of history and scholarship, on one side, and the pronouncement of faith, on the other, is complete and total. The historicity and integrity of the text of the Qur'ān stands absolutely beyond question.

Muḥammad proclaimed, and the Qur'ān (7:156–57) confirmed, what his contemporaries already knew, namely, that he was illiterate, and could not have composed the Qur'ān. The words and verses of the Qur'ān must have come to him from an outside source, which revelation identified as the Angel Jibrīl (Gabriel), the messenger from heaven. Thus Muslims believe the Qur'ān to be verbatim revelation. The Prophet's consciousness was the recipient, a passive patient that suffered the divine words to be indelibly impressed upon it. "The prophet as tape-recorder" is a theory of prophecy which Jeremiah proclaimed for the first time in the history of the Hebrew prophets and which Islam seconded and fulfilled par excellence.[12] The very word of God is "put in the mouth" of the prophet.[13] It is like a "ball of fire" which, having come, cannot but be conveyed by the prophet to the people in all its power and holiness.[14] In vain did Jeremiah warn against those who "stole" the word of God, tampered with it, or those who would "use their tongues and say, He saith." [15] In an identical, yet more emphatic vein, the Qur'ān proclaimed: "And thus have We bestowed from on high this [divine writ]. . . . We have sent it down as an Arabic Qur'an. . . . in the Arabic tongue, clear and precise. . . . Thus, when We recite it, follow thou [Muḥammad] its wording. . . . Move not thy tongue in haste, [repeating the words of the revelation:]. . . . Had the Prophet ascribed to Us anything which We did not reveal, We would have seized him by his right hand and cut off the arteries of his heart." [16]

Golden mosaics in the dome of the Great Mosque in Cordoba (965-970).

The Muslims took the revelation in dead earnest. They regarded the Qur'ān holy and divine both in its meaning-content and in its language and form. They held it in the highest honor possible. To express their esteem of it, they invented the arts of Arabic calligraphy, manuscript illumination, and book-making, arts that gave to humanity its noblest and richest creations in the visible aesthetics of the word.

Earlier revelations in the Semitic stream of history were codes of law composed in mundane and practical prose. The later revelations were narrations and exhortations to piety and virtue, but were similarly composed in plain commonsensical style. The Hebrew Old Testament contains many passages of exquisite literary beauty. But no one who believes in the divine source of the Hebrew Bible has rested his claim for its divinity on its literary beauty. On the contrary, appreciation of any literary beauty was a consequence of faith in the text's divine origin. The same dependence of beauty upon faith characterizes the

Plaited Kūfī script (Basmalah). [Photo by L. al Fārūqī.]

Christian view that the Bible – whether Hebrew, Greek, or English – is the word of God. When faith in the divine origin is absent, or when "divine origin" is understood as meaning inspiration not unlike the inspiration of human genius in poetry and letters, the common view is that the King James version, with its Elizabethan penchant for flowery language and rhymed prose, has added considerably to the literary beauty of the Hebrew Bible.

The case of the Qur'ān is the reverse of that of the Bible. Without a doubt, the Qur'ān is beautiful, indeed, the most beautiful literary composition the Arabic language has ever known. Its beauty, however, is not the consequence of faith but its very cause. The aesthetic judgment – that the Qur'ān is beautiful, nay, sublime – is not a pronouncement of faith. It is a critical judgment, reached through literary analysis. Hence, its beauty is not only held by Muslims but also by non-Muslims conversant with the literary aesthetics of the Arabic language. Instead of beauty depending upon the divine origin and flowing out of faith in that origin, the divine origin of the Qur'ān is the reasoned consequence of its literary beauty. Beauty is the cause and evidence for its divine origin. Islam is unique among the religions of humankind in that it rests the veracity of its scripture (the claim that it is revelation) on the fact of its sublime beauty. It trusts the judgment of the critical mind, familiar with Arabic literary beauty, to acquiesce unconditionally to the Qur'ānic claim upon presentation.

Indeed, this was the argument raging between the Prophet and his opponents in Makkah. The Prophet called upon them to abandon the false gods of Makkah and the debauched style of life of its people, and claimed for his call the very authority of God. It is God Himself, the Prophet claimed, Who sent the revelation commanding this radical change. Reluctant to forsake their gods, to abandon their traditions and alter their customs, the Makkans resisted. They denied the authority of the new teaching, alleging that rather than God, the source and author of the Qur'ān was Muḥammad or some teacher from whom the

Calligraphy design, Kūfī script, sixteenth century C.E.*, written in gold and black ink. The text is Qur'ān 112:1-4. [Photo by L. al Fārūqī.]*

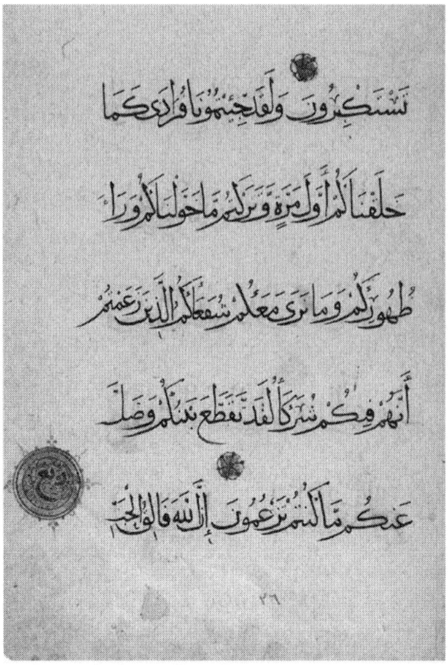

This calligraphic fragment includes verses 93-95 of the 6th chapter of the Qur'ān entitled al-Anʿam (The Cattle), in Muhaqqaq script. Date 14th-15th centuries.

Prophet borrowed these words. The so-called word of God or revelation was not divine but human, all too human, and hence devoid of commanding authority. What proof did Muḥammad have that it was divine? Could he produce a miracle such as Moses and Jesus had performed?[17] The Qur'ān answered them that he was unable, that he commanded no superhuman power, and that in the process of revelation, he was a passive patient receiving what was given by the divine source.[18] The proof that the Qur'ān was the word of God devolved upon the Qur'ān itself. It constituted its own proof by its inimitability, its superior beauty, and its moving appeal which no human composition can match. Thus, the Prophet seems to have argued, with the revelation's own backing, that the Qur'ān is divine because it is beautiful. The veracity of Muḥammad, of his call or religion, as well as that of its supporting base, the Qur'ān – that the Qur'ān is indeed revelation from God hung by a single thread, namely, the beauty of the Qur'ānic text. The Qur'ān, Muḥammad claimed with Qur'ānic approval, indeed dictation, is so beautiful that it is inimitable; it is so inimitable that it is miraculous. It is therefore not the work of humans but of God. This character of the Qur'ān is called its *iʿjāz*.

The opponents of the Prophet in Makkah sought to repudiate the claim of this inimitability, and to affirm that the Qur'ān was a human product that could be imitated and even surpassed. The Qur'ān provoked this defiance further by inviting the opponents to produce a similar book,[19] ten *suwar* like any in the Qur'ān.[20] But none would rise to the bait, despite the fact that the Arabs regarded themselves the pinnacles of poetry and literary eloquence, and the Makkans, the very head of that pinnacle. The Qur'ān reduced the challenge, asking them to produce even one *sūrah* like any of the Qur'ān whose short *suwar* had fewer than thirty words, and inviting them to bring their own gods to help.[21] The terrible struggle which the Makkans waged against Muḥammad, with all its cost in blood and injury, in tribal division and hatred, in economic hardship, in its threat to Makkah's leadership of Arabia, could have been stopped and finished by a Makkan victory if they could only compose a few verses that would equal or surpass the Qur'ān in literary beauty and eloquence.

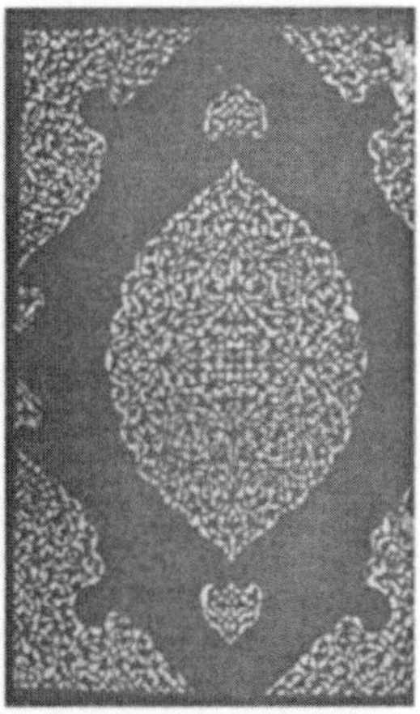

Leather-tooled Qur'ān cover, held in the Library of Sulymāniyyah Complex, Isṭanbūl. Dated 1025/1616. [Courtesy Ministry of Culture and Tourism, Government of Turkey.]

If the Makkan poets and literati were frightened by the prospect of such competition, Makkan leadership was not. Poets and men of letters from all over Arabia were called to the rescue and were promised the greatest prizes for their compositions. One of them, al Walīd ibn al Mughīrah, listened to the Qur'ān recited by the Prophet and felt admiration for it. Abū Jahl, the Makkan leader, approached him to bolster his resistance and promised him the wealth of Makkah. Al Walīd listened again to the Qur'ān and spoke out without hesitation: "I am the first connoisseur of poetry and letters in Arabia, and I speak with unquestionable authority. This Qur'ān is not the work of humans, nor of *jinn*. It has a very special beauty, a very special ring. It is replete with light and beauty, surpassing everything known." Abū Jahl insisted still more. Under pressure, al Walīd finally declared that the Qur'ān was extraordinary but human, the work of magic, not God; but that it was inimitable just as the Prophet had claimed.[22] Other poets and contenders presented their compositions as well, only to be declared failing by one another and their own sponsors. By its words, the Qur'ān wielded an awesome power, fascinating, shattering, composing, and moving. Whatever their predicament or social position, those who heard it and apprehended its meanings fell prostrate before the divine presence it signified.

The Freezing of the Arabic Language and of Its Categories

Being the verbatim word of God, the Qur'ān was the object of the greatest veneration by Muslims. It signified the divine presence itself and commanded the greatest honor. The first and perennial duty of every Muslim was to appropriate it. To memorize it, to recite its verses, to analyze its sentences and grasp their meanings – these were for the Muslim the deeds with the greatest merit. The non-Arabic speaking converts to Islam applied themselves to learning Arabic with all the earnestness of which they were capable. Many of them mastered it better than the Arabs. Too numerous to count were the non-Arab poets, prose writers, critics, and men of letters who stood at the pinnacle of Arabic literary achievement. And many more were those who contributed in major and significant ways to the elaboration and establishment of Arabic grammar, syntax, lexicography, and literary criticism. Without them, the Arabic legacy would not be itself. The Muslim Arabs, for their part, found the propagation of their mother tongue a great blessing and honor conferred upon them by the advent of Islam. To belong to the people of Muḥammad, to speak his tongue, to think in the language of the Qur'ān was an honor they guarded most avidly. To be closer to Arabic and hence to the Qur'ān meant for all Muslims to be closer to God. This caused the Muslims to preserve Arabic, to make it the language of daily discourse in order to maintain and increase their familiarity with its idioms, its figures of speech, its eloquence, the more to appreciate the beauty of the Qur'ān.

The fact that the Qur'ān was assumed to be the very word of God produced another very grave and significant result. Since the Qur'ānic word is divine, it is eternal and cannot change. Muslims may not allow their usage of it to change. Otherwise, the cumulative effect of change would alienate them from the Qur'ān to the point of rendering it liable to misunderstanding. The Qur'ānic words should be attached to their meanings forever if they are to be eternal. Otherwise, they would be dated human conventions that become obsolete as soon as their meanings shift in the flux of time and space. Rather than conveying something eternal, they would then point to something that once was and is no more. They would lose their normativeness, as human interest in them becomes academic and historical.

This issue was at the root of the controversy that raged under al Ma'mūn (197–217/813–833) when he appointed Ibn Abū Du'ād as chief justice. That jurist belonged to the Muʿtazilah school, which held the Qur'ān to be the created word of God because it feared that the contrary (namely that the Qur'ān is the eternal word of God) would compromise the divine unity. Ibn Abū Du'ād used his position to promote this view, and he was opposed by Aḥmad Ibn Ḥanbal (240/855), who led a popular resistance against the Muʿtazilah position. The opposing populace correctly perceived that to declare the Qur'ān created is to subject it to space and time and all the conditioning of history, to divest it of its holiness and thus to liberate Muslim consciousness from its determining power and normativeness. The upshot was the downfall of the Muʿtazilah school and repudiation of its doctrine. The Qur'ān emerged victorious, and the masses accepted it as uncreated not only in its meaning or content but also in its form, in the Arabic words in which it is composed. Every idea of translating the Qur'ān was laid to rest as every Muslim regarded learning Qur'ānic Arabic as the paramount religious duty. In handling its words and phrases, the Muslim believed he was in contact with the divine.

Map 19. Al Madīnah al Munawwarah and Vicinity.

A third implication of the conviction that the Qur'ān is the word of God was that the Qur'ān objectified all the norms of the Arabic language. The rules of grammar and syntax, of conjugation of words, of literary construction and beauty, in short, all that is constitutive of the language, was there, concretized in the Qur'ān as it had never been before. It was from the Qur'ān that the Arabist derived his grammar, the linguist his morphology, the poet his figures of speech. It was the standard and norm of all that pertains to Arabic. Some pre-Islamic poetry, common sayings and proverbs, a few narratives of history, or

Leather-tooled Qur'ān cover, held in the Library of Sulymāniyyah Complex, Isṭanbūl. [Courtesy Ministry of Culture and Tourism, Government of Turkey.]

passages of famous oratory survived. Where these deviated from the Qur'ān, the Qur'ānic form overruled. A total coalescence took place between the Qur'ān and the Arabic language. Thus attached to the Qur'ān as its sublime instance, the Arabic language passed beyond the flux of time and became as eternal and unchangeable as the Qur'ān itself, its ideal exemplification. Indeed, the Muslim mind never permitted any separation of the Qur'ān from its Arabic language. Arabic was nothing else besides the language of the Qur'ān. The two were equivalent and convertible since neither was possible without the other. Both remained alive, always co-present and mutually reinforcing each other. To learn the one meant to live and think in the other. To possess and understand the one was to possess and understand the other. Both remained alive as well as interdependent. Arabic could not change. It stood beyond history, beyond change. Its words and lexicography, its structure and order, its forms and norms, all froze and became immune to change. Fourteen centuries after the revelation of the Qur'ān, anyone with an average knowledge of Arabic can understand the Qur'ān as clearly and certainly as its audience did when it was first revealed. Between the Arabic-speaking Muslim and the Qur'ān there can be no ideological gap brought about by change in language or shifting of the categories of thought embedded in it. All those who know the Arabic language stand the same chance of understanding the Qur'ān as the Prophet's contemporaries had done. The only difference between them lies in the extent of one's vocabulary. Given a dictionary, their understandings must be equal if their mastery of Arabic grammar

Contemporary Kuwait mosque.

and syntax is assured. That is why understanding of the Qur'ān knows of no hermeneutical problems such as affect the Bible. The only hermeneutic the Qur'ān knows is lexicographic; the only possible question concerns the meaning a given word had at the time of revelation, which the word is then assumed to have throughout the fourteen centuries.

Calligraphy arabesque (Qur'ān 13:28). [Photo by L. al Fārūqī.]

The Ideological Content of The Qur'ān

The "How" and "What" of Revelation

The Islamic revelation described itself as a message defining *"al Dīn"* or "the definitive religion." It presented its principal idea or essence, namely *tawḥīd,* as the witness of God about Himself.[23] As regards humans, Islam regarded itself as *dīn al fiṭrah,* or "innate" or "natural religion,"[24] the religion God had implanted in humankind as He endowed them with cognitive faculties with which to discern His norms or patterns in all fields of life and activity. The foregoing descriptions imply that Islam was not a new religion but an old one, indeed, the oldest, since God, in His eternity, could not but have the same description of Himself. They also imply that the same religion must have been revealed before Islam. Indeed, it was the religion of all the prophets, the religion God conveyed to Adam when "He taught him the names of things."[25] In relating itself to the previous revelations, the Islamic revelation distinguished itself as one concerned with the norms of religion and ethics, a figurization *in abstracto,* a statement of principles and patterns. Unlike the previous revelations of the Semitic legacy which, as we saw earlier, were revelations of the law, the divine will in prescriptive form, the Islamic revelation focused on principles; and it relegated to man the task of translating them into guides and precepts for daily action and living. These guides were designated as *sharīʿah* (law) or *minhāj* (program). The revelation acknowledged,

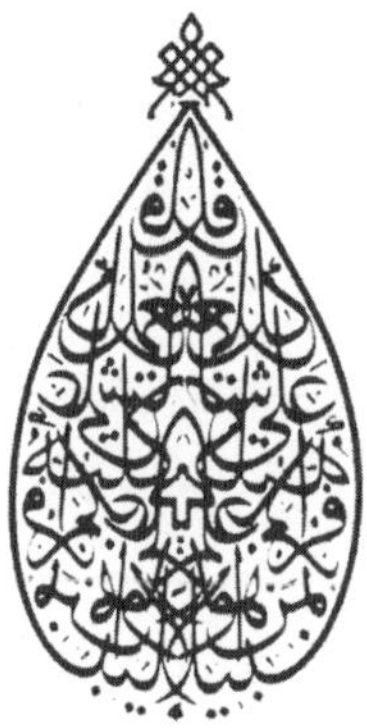

"Mirrored" calligraphy design (Qur'ān 17:84). [Photo by L. al Fārūqī.]

further, that the law is susceptible to change in time and place, conditioned as it must be by the status quo of the addressees. The needs of various societies must determine the nature of the laws they may be expected to observe. The principles of the law and its ends, on the other hand, stand above change and must remain the same throughout creation, since they represent the ultimate purposes of the Creator.

This self-view of the Islamic revelation enabled it to explain the repetition of messages from God in history. The revealed prescriptions of the past were corrupted or outgrown. They had to be superseded by new revelations responsive to the changed needs of their respective societies. That is why every society must have received more than one revelation, each progressively different from the other as far as it addressed specific prescriptions to specific circumstances of a given society, but all of them identical as far as the ultimate purposes of first principles are concerned. Revelation was a process of revocation *(naskh)* of the old law, and promulgation *(tashrī')* of the new. Hence, the succession of the prophets.

The same need for restatement has affected the divine purpose or first principles whenever the message, figurized in a language for the benefit of a specific society, fell into misunderstanding and misinterpretation. This might have been caused by change in language, or the massive migration of people, or both, rendering the meanings of the message unreachable. By suffering change, both the "what" and the "how" of the past divine messages necessitated the repetition of prophecy as God's means of communication with humanity.

The Islamic revelation separated the "what" from the "how." The latter became the prerogative of humans. They were the trustees expected to undertake the elaboration of the law and to maintain its relevance for all times and places by developing it as the varying circumstances of societies dictated. However, if this effort of humans is not to issue eventually in completely different religions, there must be an immutable statement of the core, of religious and ethical principles, which everybody can refer to as the ultimate basis of all legislation. Such a statement is precisely what the Qur'ān purported itself to be. It is the sole and ultimate authority, containing all the first principles of creation, of human life. Unlike the *sharīʿah,* which is subject to change (and necessarily so), the Qur'ān was meant to provide continuity and identity. That is why the text of the Qur'ān, as well as the cognitive tools necessary for its understanding (the Arabic language with all its principles and structures, the categories of thought imbedded in it, its words, their forms and meanings) had to be frozen, had to remain the same throughout the centuries. The Qur'ān's view of itself as the verbatim word of God, and the attachment of the Arabic language to the divine word as something inextricable from it, fit well into this overall divine scheme.

The doors of the Kaʿbah, Makkah, and its embroidered, calligraphy-design cover.

Many thinkers have wondered how it came about that all the parts of the divine scheme fitted so well together. Some have speculated that the growth of the Arabic language to its level of perfection and precision, the addiction of the Arabs to the appeal of the word, the fulfillment of their genius in the aesthetics of poetry and literary eloquence, were stages in an unfolding *Heilsgeschichte.* The question of the divine choice of placing the definitive revelation in Arabia where the situational context fitted the purpose had been raised and answered in the Qur'ān. "God knows best where to place His message" was the answer of faith. But it is also an item of the faith that God operates through material and situational causes, a fact that legitimizes the above-mentioned speculation as a fallible attempt by humans to grasp more penetratingly the nature of the divine mission.

Ideational Structure

Although the Qur'ān is indeed an ideational figurization of the essence of Islam couched in sublime Arabic form, not every word of its text pertains to that essence in the same degree and belongs, as it were, on the same level of priority. Disparity of importance between its constitutive ideational elements is due in part to its comprehensiveness. "We have not left out anything in this Book" (Qur'ān 6:38). If the book is to include everything, it must order them differently because by nature they do not all belong to the same rank. Second, the Qur'ān contains principles of religion and ethics as well as prescriptive legislation for everyday living. Some of these prescriptions have a place in the Qur'ān because of the capital importance of their content for the overall divine plan. These are the Qur'ānic laws of marriage and divorce, of dependence and inheritance. They govern the family, an institution which Islam treats with a seriousness as if it were of the essence of human life. Since human life is not possible without the institution of the family, the regulations governing its formation and dissolution, its proper development and functioning, its growth and felicity, are equally of the essence. Other Qur'ānic laws were given as illustrative of the legislation to be made by man on the basis of Qur'ān-given principles. Such are the laws pertaining to the organization of society. That society and social order and human relations must be ordered in justice and equity to all is of the essence. But the forms social order may take can and do vary. The Qur'ān's pronouncements in this regard are conditionally normative, in contrast to those first principles such as *tawḥīd,* justice, human freedom and responsibility, and so on, which are absolute and universal.

One must keep in mind that the Qur'ān does not treat its subject matter systematically. Fulfilling a requisite of the aesthetic sublime in letters, a subject to be examined below, the Qur'ān is a book in which principles and precepts are strewn like a string of pearls that has become unfurled. The ordering of its chapters, and of its verses in the chapters, is not meant to give the Qur'ān a topical structure. The order given by the Prophet on instruction from the Angel, which Muslims have always regarded as essential to the Qur'ān, fulfills the condition of the literary sublime in Arabic and most legacies of Semitic literatures. It is not developmental, not organic; it does not work itself toward a culmination or conclusion at specific points. Rather, it is composed of a series of clusters of verses, each cluster treating a different topic, but constituting a complete unit even if it is only one or two lines. As a whole, the Qur'ān is a book without beginning or end. It can be read or recited by beginning at any verse and stopping at any verse. It is infinite, or rather, a window to the infinite, a window through which the reader can peek at the supernal plenum, the infinite space of values and principles constituting the divine will.[26] Any systematization such as we have attempted in our analysis of the essence of Islam is the outcome of fallible endeavor.

At the very center of the Qur'ān's edifice of ideas stands God, the Absolute, the One, the Transcendent, the Creator, the Cause and Judge of all. His existence, His nature, His will and His creation, His purpose for humanity and His conveyance of that purpose and will through all the prophets including Muḥammad, the last of the prophets, constitute the content of the faith, the *ʿaqīdah* of Islam.

Calligraphy design by Ṣādiqayn (Qur'ān 55:26-28). [Photo by L. al Fārūqī.]

Surrounding this center of Qur'ānic ideas about the divine being and its relevance to creation is a body of methodological principles governing man's response to divinity. In their sum, these principles establish a worldview constituted by the following:

1. Rationalism or the subjection of all knowledge, including religious knowledge, to the dictates of reason and common sense, the repudiation of myth, of paradox, of ultimately contradictory positions, acquiescence to proof and evidence, and openness to further evidence and readiness to alter one's knowledge and attitude according to the demands of new evidence.

2. Humanism, or the doctrine, first, that all humans are born innocent, there being neither original sin nor guilt; second, that they are free to determine their individual destinies since neither matter nor social order can or should restrict their movement or efforts to order their lives in accordance with the best dictates of their own consciences; third, that they are equal before God and the law since no discrimination is legitimate that bases itself upon race, color, language, inherited culture, religion, or inherited social position; fourth, that they are all by nature capable of making judgments of truth and falsehood, of good and evil, of desirableness and its opposite, since without such

Muslim schoolboys with books and bone slates in the Republic of China.

capacity for judgment and action, neither humanity nor moral merit nor demerit are possible; fifth, that they are all responsible, certain to be accountable and will receive from their Creator, whether in this world or the next, exactly what their deeds have earned for them.

3. World- and life-affirmation, or the doctrine that God created life to be lived and not denied or destroyed, and the world to be enjoyed; that Creation is subservient to man, malleable and transformable by him according to his wishes and design; that both life and the world are to be promoted and developed, culture and civilization to be nurtured and to issue in human self-realization in knowledge, in *taqwā* and *iḥsān* (piety and righteousness), and in beauty.

4. Societism, or the doctrine that man's cosmic value lies in his membership in and contribution to human society; that his individual self is certainly an end-in-itself, yet more ennobled, and hence conditioned, by its subjection to humanity as an end-in-itself.

Beyond these methodological principles, but lying within the essence of the Qur'ānic figurization, is a body of ethical principles sometimes given explicitly and sometimes to be inferred from their concrete instantiations narrated or described by the Qur'ān. They constitute Islam's personal and social ethics, the moral precepts to guide the conduct of individuals and groups. The Qur'ānic text is, in the main, a phenomenology of moral values or precepts.

Finally, the Qur'ānic essence includes the institutions of Islam. These cover all fields of human activity: the religious and the ethical, the political and the economic, the cultural and the educational, the judicial and the military, as we shall have occasion to see below.

NOTES

1. As indicated by "The Prologue" and "The Epilogue" of the Code of Hammurabi, J. Pritchard, *Ancient Near Eastern Texts* (Princeton, N.J.: Princeton University Press, 1955), pp. 164–165 and 177–180, respectively.

2. Qur'ān 87:18–19.

3. John Bright, *A History of Israel* (London: SCM Press, 1960), pp. 62–63; George E. Mendenhall, "Covenant Forms in Israelite Tradition," *The Biblical Archeologist* 17 (1954), pp. 58–60; Stanley B. Frost, *Patriarchs and Prophets* (Montreal: McGill University Press, 1963), pp. 15–16.

4. H. H. Rowley, *The Growth of the Old Testament* (London: Hutchinson University Library, 1960), pp. 30–31.

5. Ibid; H. Wheeler Robinson, *The Old Testament: Its Making and Meaning* (London: University of London Press, 1961), p. 189.

6. Bright, *A History of Israel,* pp. 374–375; Rowley, *The Growth of the Old Testament,* pp. 34–36; Nehemiah 8. The redactor's insistence that intermediaries were used to "cause the people to understand the law," "to understand the reading" as Ezra was reciting it to them, suggests that the law (scripture) Ezra carried with him from Babylon (Ezra 7:14) was not in Hebrew but in some language the people could not understand (Nehemiah 8:7–8).

7. "Until the Council of Jamnia [c. 90 C.E.] . . . it is improper to speak of them [certain books which were venerated but which cannot be identified with any certainty] as a Canon." So writes H. H. Rowley, and he quotes Oesterley, Robinson, and Holscher approvingly.

8. ʿAlī ibn Ḥazm, *Kitāb al Faṣl fī al Milal wal Niḥal* (Cairo: Mu'assasat al Khānjī, 1321/1903), Vol. II, p. 22.

9. Pritchard, *Ancient Near Eastern Texts,* pp. 163–164.

10. Labīb al Saʿīd, *Al Muṣḥaf al Murattal* (Cairo: Dār al Kātib al ʿArabī, 1387/1967), pp. 68–69; ʿAbdullah ibn Abū Dawūd al Sijistānī(d. 316/930), *Kitāb al Maṣāḥif (Cairo:* Al Maṭbaʿah al Raḥmaniyyah, 1355/1936).

11. William Muir, *The Life of Muḥammad* (Edinburgh: John Grant, 1923), p. xxviii.

12. Qur'ān 53:4; 38:70; 18:110; Jeremiah 23:29–30.

13. Qur'ān 18:110, 14; Jeremiah 5:14.

14. Jeremiah 23:29.

15. Jeremiah 23:31.

16. Qur'ān 20:113; 12:2; 26:195; 75:18; 75:16; 69:44–46.

17. Qur'ān 17:90–93.
18. Qur'ān 41:6.
19. Qur'ān 52:34.
20. Qur'ān 11:13.
21. Qur'ān 17:88.
22. Muḥammad ibn Isḥaq (151/769) and Muḥammad ibn Hishām (218/834), *Sīrat al Nabiyy Ṣallā Allahu ʿAlayhi wa Sallam,* edited by M. M. ʿAbd al Ḥamīd (Cairo: Muḥammad ʿAlī Ṣubayḥ, 1383/1963), Vol. I, pp. 174–175. The event was confirmed by revelation in Qur'ān 74:11–31.
23. Qur'ān 3:18.
24. Qur'ān 3:19; 30:30.
25. Qur'ān 2:31.
26. The implications of the Qur'ānic commands to various aspects of thinking and living were elaborated in I. R. al Fārūqī, *Tawḥīd: Essays on Life and Thought* (Kuala Lumpur: A.B.I.M., 1982).

The Sunnah

The Textual Base

THE BURDEN PLACED UPON MAN BY THE ISLAMIC REVELATION, namely, henceforth to translate the *data revelata* into laws or precepts for action, was a heavy one indeed. At least in the stream of Semitic religious consciousness, it was the first time that law was desacralized – and by religion itself; it was divested of its holiness as direct revelation. Henceforth, law was declared to be a human responsibility in the exercise of which humans were fallible. When done right, law is man's greatest accomplishment; when done wrong, his greatest downfall. At any rate, law-making was to be a human activity, capable, like every other human activity, of being right or wrong. When wrong, it is equally man's responsibility to discover the locus of error, to amend that law, and bring it into accord with the divinely given principles of which the law is the translation. Certainly it is an act of mercy that God chose to aid man in fulfillment of this obligation when He provided him with an example and clarification, an exegesis of the general principles of the revelation. For that is precisely what the *sunnah* is.

Technically, the *sunnah* is a collection of the Prophet's sayings and deeds. It includes his opinions about matters good or evil, desirable or otherwise, as well as the practices of which he approved as becoming for Muslims to follow. The *sunnah* quotes the words and phrases attributed directly to the Prophet or to his companions who witnessed his attitudes and deeds and reported them. Every unit of the *sunnah* conveying a report about the Prophet is called a *ḥadīth*. The *sunnah* occupies a place second to the Qur'ān. Its function is to clarify the Qur'ān's pronouncements, to exemplify and illustrate its purposes. Where the Qur'ānic statement is general, the *sunnah* particularizes it to make it applicable; and where particular, the *sunnah* generalizes it in order to make possible its extrapolation to other particulars. The *sunnah* was first memorized by the companions of the Prophet as many of them found the time to record the Prophet's sayings in writing. Afraid that the new Muslims might confuse the word of God with the word of Muḥammad, the Prophet had first prohibited the writing down of his own sayings. Later, when the possibility of confusing the two was removed by the majority's memorization of the Qur'ān, the Prophet permitted his companions to write the *sunnah*. Among those companions who recorded some parts of the *sunnah* were Sa῾d ibn ῾Ubādah al Anṣārī (15/637), ῾Abdullah ibn Abū Awfā, Samrah ibn Jundub (60/680), Jābir ibn ῾Abdullah (78/698), Wahb ibn Munabbih (114/732) who inherited the collection of Abū Hurayrah (58/678); ῾Abdullah ibn ῾Amr whose writing recorded 1,000 or more *ḥadīth* preserved in the *Musnad* of Ibn Ḥanbal; and ῾Abdullah ibn ῾Abbās (69/589) who left us a "camel load" of writing materials covered with *ḥadīth* of the Prophet. Besides these, there was the covenant of Madīnah, the constitution of the first Islamic state and the first constitution ever to be written. Dictated by the Prophet, its principles have remained operative throughout Islamic history. The main bulk of the *sunnah,* however, was not written until later. The first generation of Muslims memorized the sayings of the Prophet, taught them to one another, observed what they prescribed, and emulated what they described as the practice of Muḥammad.

The value of the *sunnah* and its relevance to Islam was universally recognized by all Muslims. The need for it to help the Muslim fulfill the requirements of his faith in liturgical, legal, ethical, social, economic, political, and international affairs was felt by all. Hence, the *sunnah* came to be regarded, from the beginning, as a second authoritative source of Islam, whose dicta were binding on all Muslims. The Qur'ān commanded obedience to the Prophet and equated that obedience with obedience to God.[1] It ordered the Muslims to refer their disputes to him and to abide by his judgment.[2] The Prophet's companions, for their part, obeyed that command and voluntarily fulfilled everything the Prophet had asked of them. It was their unanimous consensus that the *sunnah* of the Prophet is normative, that its precepts are binding on all Muslims. Indeed, the Muslims had no other source to provide them with the specific rituals of worship and institutions of their faith, and to legislate for them in matters on which the Qur'ān is silent, save the *sunnah*. Naturally, there can be no contradiction between the Qur'ān and the *sunnah*. Everyone of the latter's provisions must be either confirmed or implied by the Qur'ān, whether explicitly, by a direct passage of the text, or implicitly, by a Qur'ānic principle or desideratum whose realization necessitates the provision commanded by the *sunnah*.

However, not all that the Prophet said or did, approved or disapproved of, is normative and hence obligatory for Muslims to follow. The Prophet was not superhuman or divine but a human, all too human, being. The Qur'ān repeated this fact many times, and the Prophet himself never tired of reaffirming this basic truth. As a human being he did, said, approved and disapproved of many things outside of his function as executor of Qur'ānic commands, as exemplar of the ethic of Islam, or as embodiment of the Islamic lifestyle. In this regard, Muslims distinguish between those items that issue from his prophethood and mission, and those that issue from his humanity. The former are accepted as normative without hesitation. The latter, in absence of evidence to the contrary, are treated as peculiar to him as a shepherd, tradesman, farmer, husband, general, statesman, paramedic, engineer, and so on. Muslims regard the former as normative and the latter, otherwise; and in doing so, they are backed by the Prophet himself, who acknowledged and accepted on numerous occasions the contrary counsel or action of his companions. The *sunnah*, as a technical term or source of Islamic law and ethics, includes only those items that are proven to have been meant by the Prophet to be followed and obeyed in loyalty to his divine message.

The foregoing differentiation in normativeness divided the *sunnah* into two great divisions; one containing all those items that give rise to law and obligation (*sunnah ḥukmiyyah*), and one containing all those that do not (*sunnah ghayr ḥukmiyyah*). Within the former, various degrees of normativeness were discerned following two criteria: first,

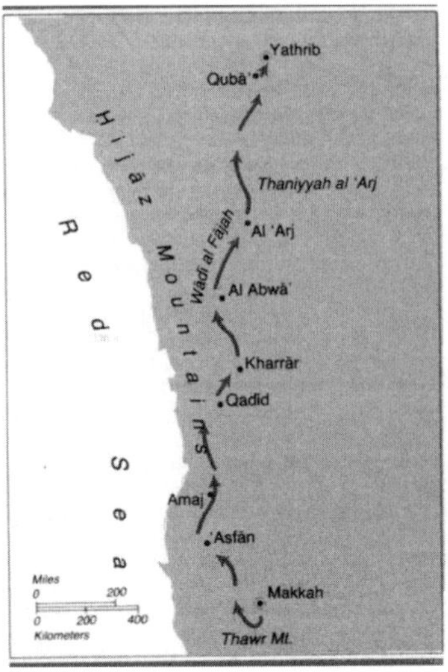

Map 20. The Prophet's Migration to Yathrib: Al Hijrah, 1/622.

the degree of certainty of provenance (*wurūd*) or the quality of our knowledge that those items issued from the Prophet and did so for the purpose of clarification or exemplification of the divine message; and second, the degree of certainty with which the specific connotation (*dalālah*), the exact identity, meaning, or form of that which is commanded, is known. This differentiation divided the *sunnah ḥukmiyyah* into *qaṭ'iyyah* (absolutely certain) and *ẓanniyyah* (probable), and these divisions applied to both provenance and connotation. Obviously, legal obligation attached only to those items fulfilling the criteria of certainty in both respects.

During the lifetime of the Prophet, the *sunnah* was for the most part something witnessed in public. As it issued from the Prophet, people heard, saw, and understood. When they were not present and sought reassurance, they could and did refer to the Prophet and asked him directly, face to face, to satisfy their quest. After his death, the companions asked one another. When all those who attended or witnessed the event agreed, their unanimity was tantamount to certainty. For it is not possible that the Prophet's companions, with all their loyalty and sincerity, their personal differences and distinctions, could come up with the same report unless the event was real and its meaning was absolutely clear. Items of the *sunnah* that fit this description were called *sunnah mutawātirah*. The *sunnah mashhūhah* refers to those items that were reported by some companions – not all – whose consensus could not have involved mistake, error, or misrepresentation; while *sunnah āḥād* includes items reported by one companion known for his good memory, fidelity, and moral integrity.

A calligraphic design ("Muḥammad" repeated 5 times) by the contemporary Turkish calligrapher Ermin Berin. [Photo by L. al Fārūqī.]

Across these divisions lies the distinction between *fiʿliyyah* (actional) and *qawliyyah* (verbal). The former refers to deeds of the Prophet, done once, occasionally, or repeatedly under the witness of the public. To this group belong the rituals and institutions of Islam which continue to be practiced throughout the Muslim world with astounding identity despite the centuries that separate their practice from the Prophet and the total discontinuity of geography, ethnicity, language, and culture among the world's followers of the Prophet. The latter comprises the Prophet's sayings heard by others and necessarily involving a lesser degree of certainty than something witnessed, unless – again like the rituals and institutions – they were repeated on a daily, weekly or yearly basis.

The *sunnah* thus was heard, witnessed, memorized, recorded, and transmitted to posterity. Since the third century A.H., it has been known through six canonical collections called the *ṣiḥāḥ* (sing. *ṣaḥīḥ*). By order of the rigor with which they carried out their sifting and classification, the collectors of the *ṣiḥāḥ* were al Bukhārī (256/870), Muslim (251/865), Abū Dā'ūd (275/888), Ibn Mājah (273/886), al Nasā'ī (303/915), and al Tirmidhī (279/892). Among these, the first two stand apart, acknowledged by all Muslims as more critical and authoritative than the rest. Those items commonly found in both their texts are most authoritative of all.

The Content

Following the death of the Prophet, the Muslims found themselves a people with a cause, a people endowed with a mission as radical as it was universal (Qur'ān 3:19, 85). The whole world had to be remade in the likeness of the divine pattern. The world within – the self – and the world without – nature – had to be transfigured into that pattern. The Muslims themselves had already undergone a radical transformation at the hands of the Prophet in the course of their conversion to Islam and their companionship with the Prophet in his lifetime. This was the justification of the name "Muslim" which revelation conferred upon them (Qur'ān, 22:78). The Prophet made certain to impart to them his

Anatolian prayer rug (eighteenth century), Turkish and Islamic Art Museum, Isṭanbūl, Turkey. [Photo by L. al Fārūqī.]

vision, his cause; and they were the excellent pupils who appropriated that vision and dedicated their lives to it. The vision of the Prophet lay complete in the Qur'ān, ready for the understanding to appropriate. The last verse to be revealed affirmed: "Today I have completed for you your religion, assigned to you My total blessing, and established Islam henceforth as your religion."[3] It signified that, as idea, principle, and representation the whole life- and worldview of Islam was complete, ready to be taken in its entirety by any intellect willing to appropriate it and possessing the minimum requisite powers of theoretical and axiological cognition. Understanding of the Qur'ān and the power to produce in oneself the self-shattering, self-reconstructing, and self-mobilizing required for joining the company of the Prophet are not readily available to all. Those who are capable of being moved by a vision presented *in abstracto* are always few; and those who, being so affected, are so moved that they cannot rest unless and until their "vision is realized in history or they perish in the process" – to use Muḥammad's own phrase – are fewer still. For, as educators have always realized, cognitive appeal presumes a strong imagination capable of representing to the consciousness a vision in the concrete where the values may exercise their appeal upon the heart with all their power. Without such imagination, the apperception remains theoretical; and theory, in the sense of ideation, does not affect the heart, the source of all movement. But, the stronger an imagination is, the more vivid its representation will be and, consequently, the more real the value represented, the stronger will be the affective emission or moving appeal. The case of the Prophet's companions could not be different from that of humanity at large. Nor could their special sensitivity to the religious and ethical plight of humankind, or their specially developed imagination as the most poetry-possessed people in the world, absolve them from the need for another aid, a nontheoretical, nonideational aid. This aid was the *sunnah*. It supplied the needed concretization of the ideal of Islam.

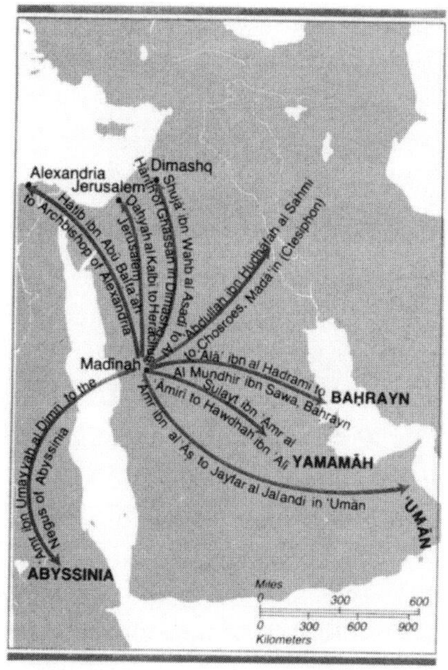

Map 21. The Prophet's Delegates to Neighboring Sovereigns, 6/628.

The *sunnah* as concretization of the vision, or materialization of the ideal, translated theory into reality. In it, the values of Islam were given form and became alive. They throbbed with moving power. In their presence, the inert became alive, lost its ontological poise, and began to move in the direction to which the values pointed. From their concrete instantiations, the values of Islam commanded the actualization of materials that fulfill their patterns; and in their presence, humans could only obey. The *sunnah* was the ministry of Muḥammad. It extended over the last twenty-two years of his life. In his life as well as after his death, the *sunnah* of Muḥammad supplied the missing link between thinking and doing, between ideational apperception and action, between thought and life and history. That is why the *sunnah* of Muḥammad became the teacher of the millions. It constituted the richest mine from which every person in a position of leadership drew to exhort or to convince, to inspire or to move. It furnished the emulatory material that dominated all Islamic celebrations, and indeed, decorated and ornamented all Muslim convocations.

The *sunnah* materials may be grouped into four categories, each of which built an image of Muḥammad in the imagination of Muslims. First were the ritualistic materials which formed the image of the Prophet as worshipper of God, as His pious servant. Second were those texts pertaining to Muḥammad's role as missionary and caller to the new faith, as a man of the world with all kinds of relations with other people of the world but living by and for his mission alone. Third were the materials pertaining to Muḥammad as a human being and hence as husband, father, relative, neighbor, and friend. Fourth were the materials pertaining to the Prophet as leader of men whether in the state, the battlefield, the marketplace, the classroom, or the mosque.

Muḥammad as Worshipper Servant of God

The principal act of worship – *ṣalāt – was* imposed by God directly on Muḥammad on the occasion of the *Isrā'* and *Mi'rāj* (the night journey to Jerusalem and ascent to heaven in the year 6 B.H./616). *Ṣalāt* is also commanded in the revelation a countless number of times, as are the other rituals of fasting, *shahādah, zakāt,* and *ḥajj*. Muḥammad taught his followers the details of *ṣalāt,* as well as of all other rituals, following the instruction given him by God. The Prophet's observance of these rituals was meticulously observed, reported, tried, and repeated in the practice of the companions. The latter performed under the eye of the Prophet who corrected every deviance from what he knew to be the norm. From the smallest detail of bodily purification to the highest spiritual meanings, these rituals constitute a fair part of the *sunnah*. Every Muslim learns them as a child, and has Muḥammad constantly in mind in his performance of them throughout his life.

A class of students performs during Commencement program at Clara Muḥammad School, Philadelphia, 1983. [Photo by L. al Fārūqī.]

Important as they certainly are for the religious life, punctuating as they do human life five times a day *(ṣalāt),* a whole month every year *(ṣiyām),* touching every unit of wealth beyond what is absolutely necessary for subsistence *(zakāt),* and providing a culmination of the Muslim's personal and corporate piety *(ḥajj),* the rituals of Islam have a restricted place. They may be neither increased, reduced, or changed because the *sunnah* has taught them in their exact and precise dimensions (or *maqādir)*. Those who flout or neglect to observe them are guilty; those who overdo and exceed the proper dimensions are perhaps not as guilty as the former, but guilty nonetheless. When asked whether it would not earn a person greater merit to fast all year and pray all night, the Prophet answered: "God did not prescribe it. . . . As for me, I pray and I sleep; I fast and I eat; I work and I keep women company." Unlike the "holy men" of other religions, Muḥammad was not therefore an ascetic denying the world and mortifying his flesh, nor a monk spending most of his hours in prayer or meditation. The rituals of Islam were acts of obedience and self-discipline, closed to indulgence of any kind. It is therefore elsewhere that we have to look for Muḥammad's pietism.

Long before any revelation came to him, the Prophet was in the habit of isolating himself and meditating over the predicament of humanity. The plight of humans everywhere distressed him; the status quo of other religions left much to be desired, for these religions had been disfigured by their guardians, the monks, priests, and rabbis. They had long since stopped to inspire and move humanity toward the great goals. And yet, the signs of God in creation were everywhere, arousing wonder and pressing the human mind to break through to its Creator. The patterns of God within the self, in the world of nature and history, were obvious if humans would only shake off the inherited stereotypes and open themselves to the ever-fresh evidence of the facts of creation.

Following revelation and Muḥammad's absolute conviction that God is, that He is indeed God, One, Absolute, Almighty, and Beneficent, he became a man possessed. Everything in the world of humans – the past, the present, the future – and everything in that of nature – the sun, moon, stars, trees, and animals big or small – moved and lived and died by God's action. Belief in God is not religious until one sees everything as the creation, work, and providence of God. Muḥammad did see the world this way and did so par excellence. Prophethood placed Muḥammad in contact with this divine Being in a special way. God was the Creator of Muḥammad and all else, as well as the Master constantly watching over and guiding everything. Above all, God as God of the universe is to be acknowledged through His works, contemplated through the events of nature and history, which fill the mind of anyone who thinks. Furthermore, He is to be loved, honored, and obeyed, not just acknowledged and held in contemplation. For what is perceived as divine is *ipso facto* understood as normative and commanding. To love, honor, and obey God is to conscript oneself voluntarily into His service, which is nothing less than transforming oneself, other selves, and the whole of creation into a harmonious whole fulfilling His will. And His will is the plenum of values, material, utilitarian, moral, religious, aesthetic. Many of these are already actualized in creation, and many others remain to be actualized by man.

This then was the meaning of worship for Muḥammad: to perceive God through His works, to acknowledge Him precisely for what He is – namely, God, the One, Absolute in all respects, ever-living, ever-present – and to fulfill His will. Worship, hence, was not something to be done at one time or place rather than another. It was a full-time occupation, a job never *accompli,* never stopped. No reason may justify a relaxation of worship except death. As long as life is, the obligation to worship continues. Such was the preoccupation of the Prophet. If he performed a ritual, he would shorten it to accommodate those observing it with him, or would lengthen it if he were alone and inclined toward contemplation. But he would never permit contemplation to disturb his penchant for the other forms of worship. He saw and heard God wherever his senses turned, and he was ever-restless in seeking to do His will.

Two examples of Indian calligraphy from the Ḥadīth literature. Both read: "Whoever builds a mosque for the sake of God, God will build for him a house in Paradise." The example on top appears on a mosque commissioned by Rukn al Dīn Barbak Shāh (fifteenth century), Hatkhola, Sylhet, Bangladesh. The one at the bottom is from a mosque in Gaur commissioned by Shams al Dīn Yūsuf Shāh (fifteenth century). [Courtesy Department of Antiquities, Government of Bangladesh.]

Muḥammad's spirituality was of a new kind. The world had known a spirituality that knew the eternal only as the antipode of the material, and sought it only at the cost of self, of world and history. Hinduism and Buddhism taught such spirituality. Such too was the spirituality of Christianity, which integrated into itself that of Alexandrian Hellenism, with all its antagonism to matter and the world. The affirmation of life, the world, and history was irreconcilable with these religions. It could be affirmed only in the pagan religions; but these were really little more than that will projected onto the supernatural and mythologized. Humanity yearned for a spirituality that would reconcile the two: a religion that affirmed life and the world but disciplined their pursuit with morality; that affirmed the personalist values of purity, faithfulness, and devotion but disciplined their pursuit with measured rituals and engagement in the making of history.

Pondering, wondering, and meditating took most of Muḥammad's energies before the Qur'ānic revelation. Thereafter, every moment of his life was an acknowledgment of God, an act of acquiescence to the Creator-Master of the universe. Every moment was an active affirmation of life, a reconstruction of culture and civilization, a remolding of the world into the divine pattern. The last two decades of his life were a continuous struggle, a constant self-exertion in the path of God. But by living in God's presence and working under His command, the struggle and exertion became rest and reassurance – the *sakīnah* which is more precious than any and all gifts. Muḥammad was in the habit of withdrawing to His Master and pleading for this *sakīnah* whenever events took a turn for the worse. But never did that recourse to God deter him from fulfilling whatever task was due, whether to himself, his family, his environment, or to the least of his people.

Muḥammad as Caller

The divine command dictated that Muḥammad should be a caller of men to God. It was to be his most solemn duty to convey the revelation to the world.[4] The command cautioned that his duty did not go beyond conveyance, that is, informing, warning, and guiding others. How the call fared, whether it succeeded or not, was not his responsibility but God's.[5] He alone disposes, guiding or not permitting to be guided whomsoever He wills.[6] In perfect obedience, Muḥammad conveyed all that was revealed to him and lost no time in calling to the new faith all those he could contact. The unique incident in his career, in which he failed to call a

At prayer (ṣalāt) in the Masjid Negara (National Mosque) in Kuala Lumpur, Malaysia. [Photo by L. al Fārūqī.]

Interior of mud mosque, Zaria, Nigeria. [Courtesy A. R. Doi.]

blind pauper to the faith because he was preoccupied by a man of influence,[7] was not a case of failure to call. For his business with the notable was equally a call to Islam. This was an error in judgment as to who was more important at that moment of time. The obligation to call, the concern for the faith quality of everyone, never left Muḥammad's consciousness. He turned every occasion into an opportunity for mission. And the image of the Prophet as *dā'iyah* or "caller to God" has commanded the imagination of Muslims ever since. In this image, and in the anecdotes and direct sayings of which it is composed, the *sunnah* concretized the vision of Islam as the valued personal quality and lifestyle of Muslims.

The Prophet was armed with the most formidable – indeed miraculous and irresistible – weapon, namely, Qur'ānic eloquence. The power of the Qur'ān to persuade and to convince was a great *tremendum,* a moving *fascinosum,* without match. As sublime presentation of Islam, the Prophet allowed it to speak for Islam on every occasion, thus giving the call the numinous power of the divine voice. Thus, when 'Utbah ibn Rabī'ah and the Quraysh tribe offered Muḥammad kingship, money, wealth, and medication, assuming that those things would cause him to desist from his opposition to Makkan religion, Muḥammad answered them with verses from the Qur'ān. Those verses did not only ward off the suspicion that Muḥammad was in search of kingship and wealth, or was sick and needed medication, but also converted the Makkan delegate, Rabī'ah, to Islam. For those who understand Arabic, the Qur'ān is truly mighty. A phrase or two of it well woven into the text of a speech or an essay could set the composition on fire, make it vibrant and penetrating. Muḥammad's speech relied heavily on the Qur'ān and often was composed exclusively of Qur'ānic verses.

Qur'ānic quotations aside, Muḥammad's own human speech was

eloquent. He used to say that, having been brought up in the camp of Banū Saᶜd bin Bakr, he spoke Arabic precisely and eloquently. He appreciated literary eloquence highly and admitted that "literary beauty is a fascinating art." Certainly, he was a master of the Arabic language, capable of manipulating it to touch the hearts of his audience and stimulate their imagination. Added to his personal conviction of God and of His attributes and actions, and to the zeal he felt in his attachment to the cause, the Prophet was preeminently successful in convincing the people of the truth. His words, as ᶜĀ'ishah has reported, were always so well measured that they were easy to memorize from the first hearing; and none had touched the strings of the heart and elicited such emotions as did Muḥammad.

Muḥammad lent his ear readily to everyone who sought it. He listened with a smile expressing sympathy, and with eyes focused on the speaker in candid interest. When his time to respond came, he did so to the point, never ambiguously. If he did not know the answer, "God knows better" was the reply. If the matter was controversial, he would reassure the speaker and win his acquiescence to the principles underlying the problem, principles that were always religious. Anyone who talked to Muḥammad emerged not only convinced of his judgment in the matter at hand but also of the greater issue, and became a new recruit for the cause of Islam. Still more, such a person emerged fully in love with and admiration for the Prophet's person. This was the case with his fiercest opponents, such as the aforesaid ᶜUtbah ibn Rabīᶜah and ᶜUmar ibn al Khaṭṭāb.

Piligrim in prayer. [Courtesy Saudi Arabian Ministry of Information.]

The latter drew his sword in rage over the Prophet's "blasphemies" against the gods of the Quraysh, and went looking for

Muḥammad to put an end to this scourge once and for all. That very trip ended in his conversion to Islam, and he became one of its staunchest defenders. The Qur'ān and Muḥammad's call vanquished the voice of paganism in 'Umar and replaced it with the voice of Islam. Muḥammad's ministry was a perfect exemplification of the divine commandments: "Argue with them with fairer and more comely saying. . . ." "Respond to evil with good, and the enmity between you and the evil-doer will be transformed into warm friendship."[8]

Woodcarving on traditional houses of Saudi Arabia. [Courtesy Saudi Arabian Ministry of Information.]

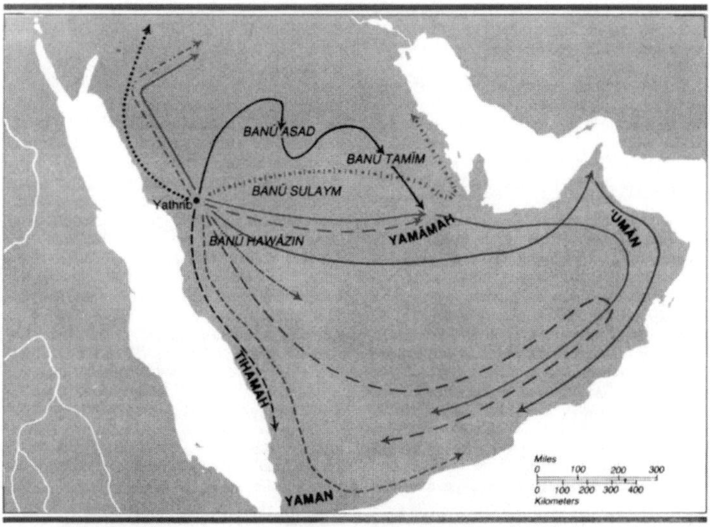

Map 22. The Riddah (Apostasy) Wars, 10-12/632-634.

COMMANDER	AGAINST
Khālid ibn al Walīd,	Ṭulayḥah ibn Khuwaylid al Asadī, Banū Asad, Bazākhah.
	Mālik ibn Nuwayrah, Banū Tamīm, Biṭāḥ
'Ikrimah ibn Abū Jahl,	Musaylimah at Yamaman
Shuraḥbil ibn Ḥasanah,	– to help 'Ikrimah and 'Amr ibn al 'Āṣ
Muhājir ibn Abū Umayyah,	al Aswad al 'Ansī 'Amr ibn Ma'dī Karib and Qays ibn Makshūḥ in Yaman
Suwayd ibn Muqrin,	to Tihāmah of Yaman(western plain) vs. Al Ḥakam ibn Ḍabī ah at Bahrayn
Al 'Alā' ibn al Ḥaḍrami,	
Ḥudhayfah ibn Muḥṣin,	Dhū al Tāj Laqīṭ ibn Mālik in 'Umān
'Arfajah ibn Harthamah,	to Mahrah
'Amr ibn al 'Āṣ,	Quḍā'ah
Ma'an ibn Ḥājiz al Sulamī,	Banū Sulaym and Hawāzin
Khālid ibn Sa'īd ibn al 'Āṣ,	to outskirts of Byzantium

The Prophet took great risks in conveying his message. The early years in Makkah brought terrible reaction. The Makkans jeered at him and his friends. They threw their refuse in his face and boycotted his whole tribe regardless of whether they were Muslims or not. Muḥammad took his call to Ṭā'if, was pelted with stones and chased away, and almost perished on that mission. His failure weighed heavily on his conscience, causing him to pray to God like one defeated but still loyal and faithful. In the service of mission, Muḥammad spared neither himself nor his companions. So great was his enthusiasm to respond favorably to any invitation to present Islam that his enemies took it as a way to fight Islam by killing its adherents. Once, he sent six of his companions to the Hudhayl tribe (Ḥijāz) at the tribe's request. At al Rajīʿ, the said tribesmen fell upon the Muslims, killed four, and sold two to Makkah. The latter were also executed. He sent a number of his dearest companions, under the protection of Abu Barā' ʿĀmir ibn Mālik, to teach Islam to the tribes of Najd. At the well of Maʿūnah, the tribesmen of Banū ʿĀmir fell upon the Muslims and decimated them. One Muslim, taken for dead among the corpses, survived to tell the story.

For the sake of this mission, Muḥammad was always prepared to forgive. He forgave all the Makkans – including those who opposed him most – and invited them to join the new faith, at the time of his greatest victory. Custom prescribed their enslavement and confiscation of all their wealth; but for Muḥammad, the higher interest of mission came first and last. Similarly, the Prophet would not execute ʿAbdullah ibn Ubayy, who had vilified and cheated him, committed treason against the Islamic state, and fought the movement on every occasion. When the son of ibn Ubayy, a fervently committed Muslim, heard that his father had been condemned by the Prophet, he asked that he be the executioner, lest somebody else's execution create in him a will to vengeance. Indeed, when ibn Ubayy died, the Prophet offered a shroud for his remains, led the funerary prayer for him, and walked in his funeral, thus convincing his son and all those who witnessed these events that propagation of the faith could and should vanquish all thoughts of retribution. Following the Muslims' victory at Ḥunayn (8/630), the Makkans helped themselves to the greater part of the war booty; when the Madīnans complained, the Prophet offered himself as compensation, saying, "Are you not the happier that the Makkans are running away with the material things and you with the Prophet of God?"[9]

Muḥammad taught every Muslim to be a missionary for Islam; and he taught them well. Whether in high or low position, missionaries emulate their prophet well. The Muslim has consistently made a commendable presentation of the message of Islam. This is partly due to the normative nature of the message and partly to the teaching of the Prophet. Jaʿfar ibn Abū Ṭālib was brought into the presence of the Negus of Abyssinia to answer the Makkan charge and request for extradition to Makkah of himself and the few Muslims who escaped thither. Jaʿfar presented the case of Islam truthfully and yet in a way that could not but win the pleasure of the king. "O King," he said, "we were in a state of ignorance and immorality, worshiping idols, eating carrion, committing all sorts of iniquities. . . . The strong among us exploited the weak. Then God sent us a prophet. . . . He called us to worship naught but God . . . to tell the truth, to hold to trust and promise, to assist the relative or neighbor . . . to avoid fornication and false witness. . . . We believed and followed him. . . . The Makkans tried to dissuade us and inflicted upon us great suffering. That is why we came hither. . . . As for Jesus, our Prophet brought us this revelation concerning him." Here Jaʿfar recited verses from *sūrah* "Maryam," which fell upon the ears of the audience like sweet music. The Negus and his Patriarchs were moved to tears and vowed never to extradite the Muslims or molest them.[10]

Muḥammad as Family Man

Muḥammad was twenty-five when someone first suggested that he should get married. He was a poor man, a dependent of his uncle Abū Ṭālib. Young men in Makkah were in the habit of frequenting its bars and flirting with the barmaids. Not Muḥammad! He led a life of chastity and purity. Nothing of the petulance of youth or the debauchery of adult life in Makkah was known of him. In the last two years of his bachelorhood, Muḥammad was in the employ of Khadījah, a widow and a merchant, whose interest he had served well enough to deserve her praise as well as that of Maysarah, her long-trusted and faithful servant. The latter went on the trading trips with Muḥammad looking after the interests of his employer. The successful ventures were as much his as Muḥammad's; but Maysarah modestly put Muḥammad ahead of himself, reporting to Khadījah that the successes were exclusively Muḥammad's.

The fact that nobody had spoken to Muḥammad about marriage indicates that marriage was not on his mind. That explains his stupefaction when Nafīsah bint Munyah, a friend of Khadījah, suggested that if he would entrust the matter to her, she would secure for him the hand of Khadījah with all the wedding expenses prepaid. Muḥammad was elated, and he and Khadījah were married. Khadījah gave Muḥammad all his children but one: Fāṭimah, who married Muḥammad's cousin ʿAlī and bore him his only grandsons, Ḥasan and

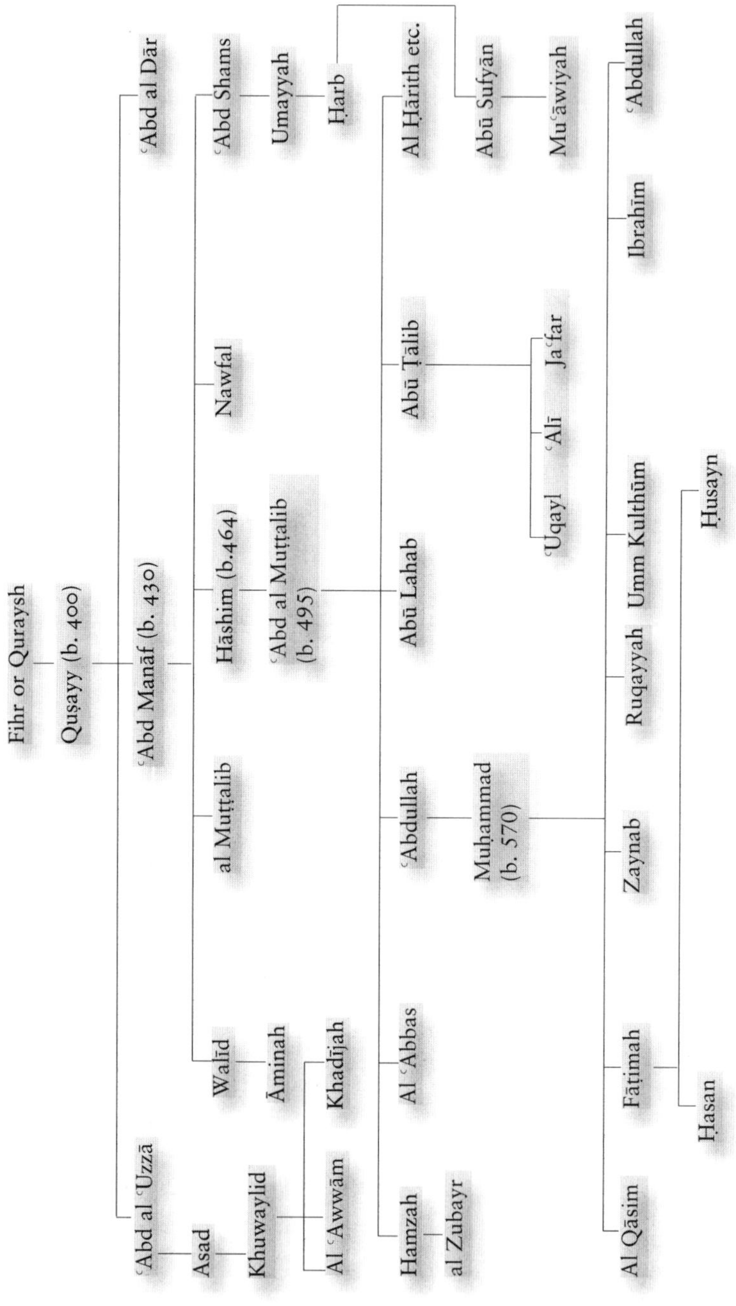

Table 6.1 Genealogy of the Prophet

Ḥusayn. Fāṭimah alone survived her father's two sons, Qāsim and Ṭāhir, who died in infancy. Three daughters, Zaynab, Ruqayyah, and Umm Kulthūm, all married and died without children before 8/630.[11] In 9/631, another son, called Ibrahīm, was born to Muḥammad from his Egyptian wife Maryam. That child also died in infancy. Khadījah remained the only wife of Muḥammad as long as she lived. Their marriage lasted until her death in 1 B.H./621. It was during this period that many of the most important events of the life of Muḥammad occurred. It was indeed a happy marriage for both.

Khadījah's wealth relieved Muḥammad of the burden of working for a living. It liberated him from material concern for himself and his family, and provided him with the leisure requisite for long meditations, one of which was the occasion for the first revelation. When those first revelations came, Muḥammad thought himself sick or possessed. He could not bring himself to believe what the Angel had conveyed to him, that he was to be a prophet. It fell to Khadījah to prop up her husband's spirits, to reassure and inspire him, to help him gain confidence in himself and in those extraordinary experiences. With the repeated return of the vision, Khadījah herself needed reassurance. She sought this from Waraqah ibn Nawfal, a distant uncle of hers, reputed for his religious knowledge and wisdom. After hearing a full report, Waraqah exclaimed, "By Him Who dominates my soul, Muḥammad is the Prophet of this nation. The great Spirit that has come to Moses has now come to him. . . . May he be firm!" Khadījah was certainly encouraged; but it was a tremendous burden that she had henceforth to carry as wife of someone who was to be a prophet. Muḥammad loved his wife dearly. He poured on her all the affection of which he was capable. He cried when she died; and he kept her memory on every occasion. Later, his youngest wife, ʿĀ'ishah said, "I have never been more envious than I am of Khadījah, long dead as she may be."

Though Muḥammad married eight times after the death of Khadījah, only one of them was a real marriage. That was his marriage to ʿĀ'ishah, daughter of his closest companion, Abū Bakr. The others were marriages for political and social reasons. The Prophet entered into them as an exemplification of a new value Islam taught. A few examples will illustrate. Zaynab bint Jaḥsh, a cousin of his whom

Table 6.2
Chronology of the Prophet's Life and Activities

570 C.E.	Abraha's abortive attack on Makkah, "The Year of the Elephant." Death of ʿAbdullah, the Prophet's father. Muḥammad's birth (August 20).
570–575	Muḥammad's nuture by Ḥalīmah and residence at Banū Saʿd. Persian conquest of Yaman. Expulsion of the Christian Abyssinians.
575–	Persecution of Christians in Yaman by the Jewish King Dhū Nuwās.
575–597	Persian dominion in Yaman
576	Death of Āminah, the Prophet's mother.
578	Death of the Prophet's grandfather, ʿAbdul Muṭṭalib.
580–590	The Fijjār War.
582	Muḥammad's first journey to Syria. Meeting with Baḥīrah.
586	Muḥammad's employment by Khadījah.
595	Muḥammad's second journey to Syria. Muḥammad marries Khadījah.
605	Muḥammad helps rebuild the Kaʿbah.
610	Call to Prophethood (June). Beginning of the revelation of the Qur'ān. Khadījah, ʿAlī, and Abū Bakr accept Islam in that order.
613	Public preaching of Islam begins. Confrontation with the Makkans.
615	Ḥamzah accepts Islam. First Muslim migration to Abyssinia. ʿUmar accepts Islam.
616	General boycott of Banū Hāshim. Return of the first emigrants.
617	Second migration of Muslims to Abyssinia.
619	Death of Abū Ṭālib. Death of Khadījah. Muḥammad seeks tribal protection and preaches Islam in Ṭā'if.
620	Muḥammad's engagement to ʿĀ'ishah bint Abū Bakr. First converts of Aws and Khazraj from Yathrib.
621	First meeting of al ʿAqabah. Al Isrā' and al Miʿrāj (night journey and ascent to heaven). Second meeting of al ʿAqabah. Attempted assassination of the Prophet by the Makkans. July 16, the Hijrah, the Prophet's migration to Yathrib, henceforth called Madīnah al Nabiyy, or The City of the Prophet, 1/1/1 A.H.

The Sunnah

1 A.H./ 622 C.E.	The Prophet builds a mosque and residence. Establishment of Islamic brotherhood as new social order. The Prophet founds the first Islamic state. The Covenant of Madīnah. Muḥammad marries ʿĀ'ishah. The call to worship (*ṣalāt*) is instituted. ʿAbdullah ibn Salām accepts Islam. The Jews attempt to split the Aws-Khazraj coalition.
1/623	Ḥamzah's campaign against the Makkans near Yanbuʿ. Campaign of al Kharrār.
2/623	Campaign against Waddān. The incident of Finḥāṣ. Campaign of Buwāṭ. Campaign of al ʿUshayrah.
2/624	Institution of Kaʿbah in Makkah as *Qiblah* (orientation) in worship. Campaign of Badr (first Muslim victory). Campaign of Banū Qaynuqāʿ.
3/624	Campaign of Banū Sulaym. Campaign of Dhū Amarr. Campaign of al Qaradah.
3/625	Muḥammad's marriage to Ḥafṣah, widow, daughter of ʿUmar.
4/625	Campaign of Ḥamrā' al Asad. Marriage of ʿAlī to Fāṭimah, the Prophet's daughter. Campaign of al Rajīʿ. Treachery against Islam at Bi'r Maʿūnah. Campain of Banū al Naḍīr.
4/626	Campaign of Uḥud; martyrdom of Ḥamzah.
5/626	First campaign of Dawmat al Jandal.
5/627	Campaign of al Muraysiʿ. *Ḥadīth al Ifk* (libel) against ʿĀ'ishah. Campaign of al Khandaq (The Ditch). Campaign of Banū Qurayẓah.
6/628	Second campaign of Dawmat al Jandal. Campaign of Fadak. Campaign of Khaybar. Al Ḥudaybiyah Peace Treaty with Makkah. The Prophet sends delegates to present Islam to the neighboring monarchs.

7/629	First Islāmic *Ḥajj*. Khālid ibn al Walīd and ʿAmr ibn al ʿĀṣ accept Islam.
8/629	Killing of Muslim missionaries at Dhāt al Ṭalḥ.
8/630	Campaign of Makkah. The Makkans accept Islam. Destruction of the idols and cleansing of the Kaʿbah. Conversion of the Arab tribes in the Ḥijāz. Campaign of Hawāzin at Ḥunayn.
9/631	Second Muslim pilgrimage (led by Abū Bakr).
10/631	Thc Christian delegation of Najrān (Yaman) visits Madīnah and is incorporated into the Islamic state as a constituent *ummah* in that state. The Year of Deputations: The Arab tribes enter Islam and pledge their loyalty.
10/632	Death of Muḥammad's son Ibrahīm. Last pilgrimage of the Prophet. Completio of the revelation of the Qur'ān.
11/632	Death of the Prophet. The campaign of Mu'tah.

Muḥammad knew well, was given by him in marriage to Zayd ibn Ḥārithah, Khadījah's slave whom Muḥammad had manumitted. Incompatibility of the spouses made them miserable, and the marriage broke down. This was a double tragedy, since Arab custom made the divorced wife of a slave a social pariah, forever unmarriable. Although this custom was abolished by Islam, no Muslim would condescend to marry the woman despite her young age. To raise her status and teach the Arabs a lesson against social stratification, Muḥammad took her in marriage. Ḥafṣah was a widowed daughter of ʿUmar ibn al Khaṭṭāb, a close companion of the Prophet. She was in her forties and was poor. Her father was even poorer. He offered her to a number of friends and acquaintances, but all declined. It grieved him deeply that his daughter was homeless, unprotected, and liable to fall into trouble. To uplift them both and teach the Muslims that it is necessary for them to give the needed protection to their single women, especially the widows, the Prophet joined her to his household as his wife.

Sawdah was the Muslim wife of Sakrān ibn ʿAmr, one of the first converts to Islam. The Prophet married the couple when Sawdah converted to Islam. She had to run away from her family to avoid their vengeance. The same had happened to her husband. The Prophet ordered them both to emigrate to Abyssinia. On their return, Sakrān died. Sawdah had to choose between staying in the streets or returning to her family and their retribution. Muḥammad had to give her the protection due and reassure his other followers that their families would not be left to the mercy of their enemies, should they fall as martyrs in the raging conflict.

Juwayriyyah was the daughter of al Ḥārith, chief of the Banū al Musṭaliq tribe. She was a widow, and she fell captive in the war her people waged against the Muslims. The Prophet took her as his portion of the booty, manumitted her in respect to her father, and offered to take her in marriage. Her father left the choice to her, and she decided in favor of Islam and marriage to Muḥammad. Her honor was thus kept. She proselytized for Islam with her people and brought them all into the faith a few months following her marriage.

These and other women were elevated through their marriage to Muḥammad to the rank of "mothers of the Believers." Each one played an important role in the formative period of Islam and contributed to the social cohesiveness of the new society. Having declared the old tribal ties illegitimate in the new universalist *ummah*, Muḥammad used every other cohesive to consolidate the fledgling society. The honor of belonging to the house of the Prophet or of being related thereto by marriage was part of the great reform Islam had introduced in man–woman relations. Prior to Islam, a woman was regarded by her parents as a threat to family honor and hence worthy of burial alive at infancy. As an adult, she was a sex object that could be bought, sold, and inherited. From this position of inferiority and legal incapacity, Islam raised

Interior, Sulaymāniyyah Mosque, Isṭanbūl, finished in 1558.

Al Awzā^c^i (d. 158/774) was the founder of the school of law known by his name. The majority of Syria, Lebanon, Jordan, and Palestine belonged to his school from 134 to 300 A.H. Beginning in 150 A.H. Abū Zar^c^ah introduced the school of Shāfi^c^ī; and that of Ibn Ḥanbal began to spread after 250 A.H. Today, the whole area is overwhelmingly Ḥanafī, a school that, having conquered Iraq from 100 A.H. on, began to spread in Syria in 150 A.H., with a sprinkling of Ḥanbalīs and Shafi^c^īs among the Sunnīs. Substantial minorities (Druze, Shi^c^ah Twelvers or Ithnā ^c^Asharis, and Seveners or Isma^c^īlīs) emerged under Fāṭimī rule and continue to the present day.
Spain was all Ḥanafī until 200 A.H. The Mālikī school became predominant by 250 A.H. and continued unchallenged until the end of Muslim rule in that country (898/1492).
India is predominantly Ḥanafī. Small Shi^c^ah minorities (mostly Isma^c^īlīs) continue to survive in the region around Bombay.

women to a position of influence and prestige in family and society. Regardless of her marital status, a woman became capable of owning, buying, selling, and inheriting. She became a legal entity whose marriage was impossible without her consent, and she was entitled to divorce her husband whenever there was due cause. All religious obligations and privileges fell equally upon women as well as upon men. Adultery being looked upon by Islam as a capital and most degrading crime, Islam protected women and guided them against all that may lead to their downfall. It exempted a woman from having to earn her livelihood by obliging her male relatives to support her at all times. It further decreed that in any matter a woman should be entitled to at least as much as she was obliged to give, and so always with kindness.

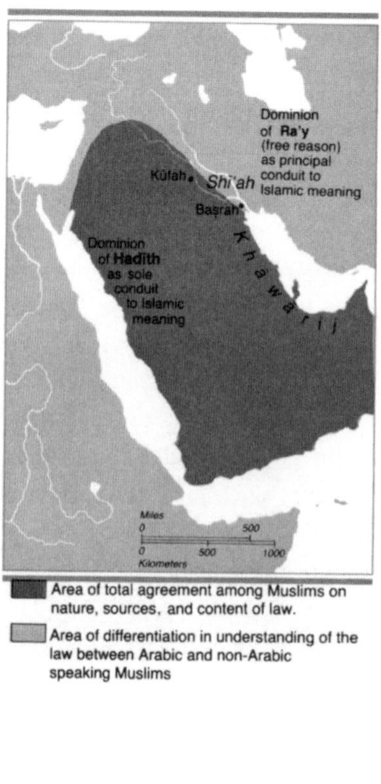

Map 23A. Law and Jurisprudence, 41-200/661-815.

All these legal reforms were radical in their day; and they remain radical in much of the world today. Muḥammad and his household provided the exemplification of these reforms, and added to it the embodiment of the new ethic. His wives testified that Muḥammad's sympathy for them never waned; that they never saw him except with a smile on his face. And they in turn made his home an abode of peace and contentment. As Prophet and head of state, he did not regard it beneath his dignity to help them in their daily house chores. On the contrary, he made them think of him as their equal. One of them was bold enough once to say to him, "Alright now, it is your turn to speak. But please say only the truth." The remark infuriated her father, ʿUmar, who was present and who castigated her severely for her offensive tone. Muḥammad interfered, saying: "We did not invite you here for this purpose." Muḥammad spent long hours with his children and grandchildren. He lengthened his prostration once in order not to push away a grandchild who saw his position as an invitation to ride on his back. He counseled his followers to be good to their families, declaring that "surely the best among you in the eye of God are the best toward their families." Muḥammad called earning a livelihood for one's dependents an act of worship and raised its value to the level of martyrdom. The Qur'ān condemned monkery (57:27), and the Prophet used to add: "Marriage is of my *sunnah.*" He encouraged the young Muslims to marry, often contributing to their dowries or reducing those obligations to affordable amounts. The Qur'ān condemned killing one's children, whether out of fear for family honor, or out of fear of poverty and famine. The Prophet urged the Muslims to procreate, saying: "Allah will provide for them"; their numbers are "pleasing to God and His Prophet."

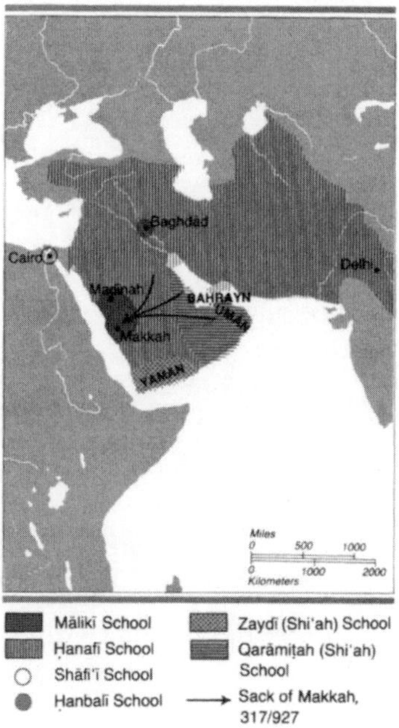

Map 23B. Law and Jurisprudence, 201-350/816-963.

This great emphasis on the necessity and value of the family coincided with the destruction by Islam of the tribe and the loyalties and

Map 23C. Law and Jurisprudence: Spread of the Schools.

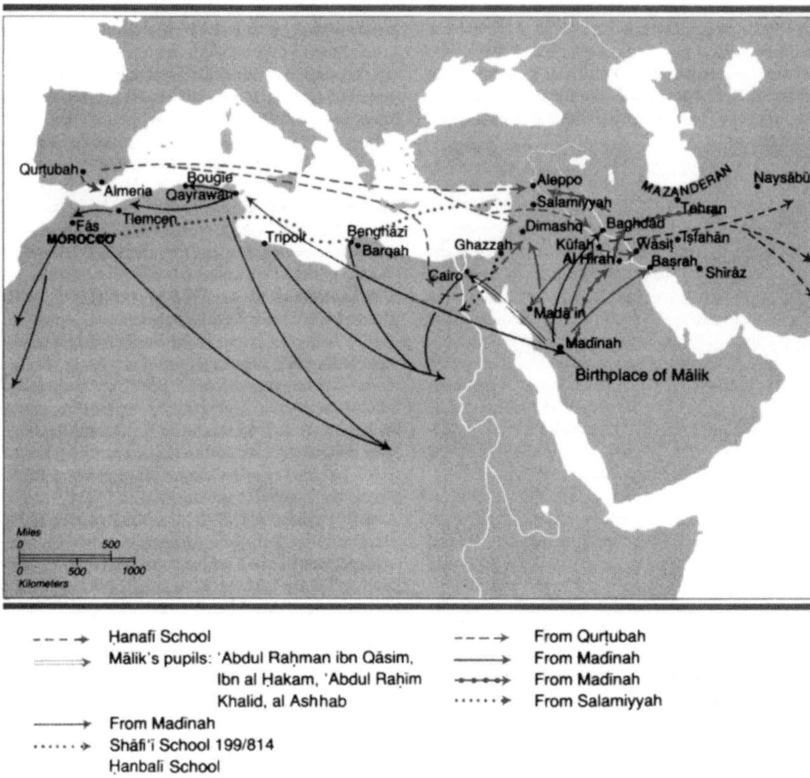

commitments to which it had given rise. First, the family was a matter of nature. Based upon the bond of blood, it harbored feelings of love, of trust, and of concern that may not be violated without injury to the human personality. Hence, Islam acknowledged and girded it with law. Second, by regulating inheritance and dependence, Islam enabled the family to exist and prosper in its extended form, so that three generations could live together and eat from the same kitchen. Third, the large membership prevented any gap from forming between the generations and facilitated the processes of socialization and acculturation of the members. Fourth, Islam made available in any household a wide variety of talents and temperaments so that the members might complement one another; and it disciplined them to adjust to one another's needs.

Beyond the family, there was only the universal *ummah*, Islam having done away with the tribe and its institutions. The *ummah* was both the universal community and the universal state. It was an open and egalitarian society which any individual or group could join by an act of decision. Unlike the world-empires which are built upon power and designed to exploit the slave and subject populations for the benefit of the elite few, the *ummah* was classless. The bond holding it together was a rational one, built upon the consensus which members shared in the vision of Islam. It depended upon education in that vision and training in its implementation on the local and universal levels. The family bond, on the other hand, is a blood call affecting humans willy-nilly, regardless of their ethical or rational maturity. Certainly, it can also rise to the level of rationality and carry some of the noblest and most ethical meanings of which man is capable. But there is no denying that without this rationality the family bond is both necessary and universal, unlike the "ummatic" bond which is exclusively acquired and rational.

Muḥammad as Leader

Perhaps the most essential quality of leadership is the capacity to perceive and to assess correctly all the factors given in a situation, to decide upon the desired objective, to design the best strategy for execution, to convince those involved of the appropriateness of the whole scheme, and to move them to desire it with the strongest will of which they are capable. Muḥammad had this capacity to a very high degree. Had there been no Islam, he would have been the ablest statesman Makkah ever knew. Islam added its own worldview as a new objective, and expanded the scope of leadership to humanity and the world.

A single event in the early *sunnah* of the Prophet gave evidence of his leadership qualities. While the Makkans were rebuilding the Kaʿbah following a flood that cracked its walls, the chieftains disputed among themselves who should have the honor of laying the cornerstone. This was the Black Stone which the Makkans had honored for generations. Since all the chiefs were involved, the suggestion of Abū Umayyah that they bind themselves to accept the arbitration of the first comer to the site, was accepted but with apprehension. When the first comer turned out to be Muḥammad, they felt reassured that his judgment would bear no prejudice to anyone. Entrusted with the task, Muḥammad decided to roll the Black Stone onto a canvas and to have each of the tribal chiefs hold on to a corner of the canvas as they carried the stone to its place. Each chief emerged satisfied that the honor was his, and that none had surpassed him in that honor. All were deeply grateful to Muḥammad who turned a threatening occasion into one full of joy.

The same astute perception of Muḥammad was present when he first arrived in Madīnah. The Muslims welcomed him warmly. Each wanted to have the honor of receiving Muḥammad in his home; and toward this end, the tribal chiefs competed with one another. The Prophet said he was not going to make a decision; rather, he would stop wherever his camel would stop. After wandering in the streets of Madīnah for a while, the camel came to rest on the empty lot of Sahl and Suhayl, the sons of 'Amr. The Prophet paid for the land and upon it built his first mosque.

Just as he would not favor one chief or section of the community over another, Muḥammad was always careful not to claim any privilege for himself. He regarded himself as an equal among equals. When mealtime approached as he marched on a campaign, his companions declared they would prepare the meal. They apportioned the tasks among themselves and left nothing for the Prophet to do. Noticing that they had omitted the collection of wood for the fire – the hardest and least pleasant chore – Muḥammad declared: "And I will gather the wood." Among subordinates, his position was that the chief should always be worthy of their love and esteem. This he expressed in the *ḥadīth* that says: "The prayer of the *imām* (leader) who is hated by the people is unacceptable to God"; "whoever assumes the leadership of a

Interior view of the Sathgumbad Mosque, Bagerhat, District Khulna, Bangladesh, c. 1459.

people against their will, his prayer never reaches beyond his ears." Neither his prophethood nor his status as chief of state prevented Muḥammad from treating others as his equals. Indeed, it was he who taught the Muslims to have their servants and slaves eat at the same table, to give them the same clothes to wear, to call them "son" rather than "servant" or "slave," and be called by them "uncle" rather than "master." One day in the marketplace, a merchant whom Muḥammad patronized took his hand and kissed it. Muḥammad pulled his hand back saying, "That is what the Persians do to their king. I am not a king, and you are not a Persian." Likewise, when the Muslims were mobilized to dig a ditch in front of the vulnerable part of Madīnah as defense against cavalry attack, Muḥammad insisted on joining them with his own hands. Long before his prophethood, this quality caused Muḥammad to be loved by his companions and acquaintances. Zayd was an adult slave brought to Makkah for sale. Khadījah bought him and presented him to Muḥammad, who manumitted him forthwith and made him his assistant. Soon Zayd's father arrived to ransom his son; but, finding him free, he offered to take him home. Muḥammad gave Zayd the choice of staying or returning to his home and family, but Zayd chose to remain with Muḥammad.

For his personal security in Makkah, Muḥammad relied on tribal loyalties. His tribe, Banū Hāshim, could and did protect him for many years against the rest of Makkah. This protection was not without its price in vituperation and ridicule, in injury and social and economic boycott. Makkan opposition was gaining momentum while Muslims were still too few and weak in Makkah. Soon, the situation became critical; and Muḥammad's tribal chief had to ask his nephew – Muḥammad – to drop the cause. But Muḥammad refused, pledging his own life to pursue the struggle to the end. Although the uncle supported Muḥammad and rejected Makkah's ultimatum, Muḥammad knew that the time of decision was near and that the men of Banū Hāshim were no match for all the Makkans now united against them because of him. It was his prescience of this situation that prompted him to negotiate and enter into two successive covenants with the Muslims of Madīnah. Thus he would replace the tribal relationship, should Banū Hāshim give up their support, and bolster his forces against the

Table 6.3 The Early Caliphs

A. *The Rāshidūn Caliphs, al Madīnah* (11–41/632–661)

	Date
Abū Bakr al Ṣiddīq	11–13/632–634
'Umar Ibn al Khaṭṭāb	13–24/634–644
'Uthmān ibn 'Affān	24–36/644–656
'Alī ibn Abū Ṭālib	36–41/656–661

B. *The Umawī Dynasty, Dimashq* (41–133/661–750)

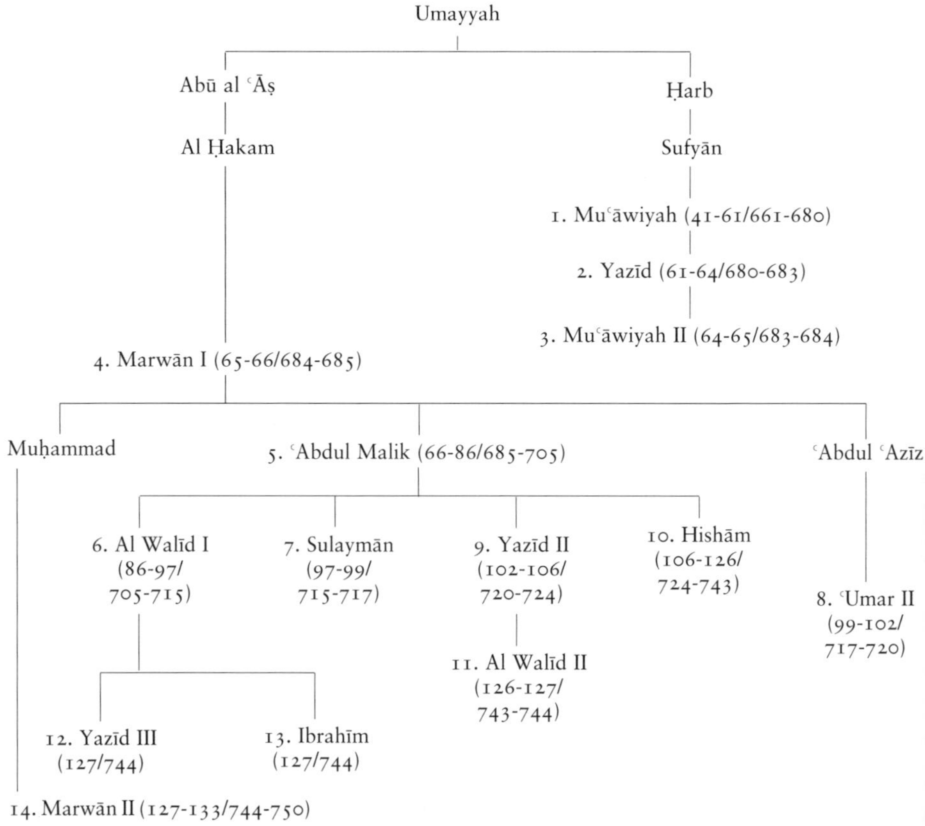

C. *The Umawī Dynasty, Qurṭubah* (139–423/756–1031)

1. ʿAbdul Raḥman I (139-172/756-788)
   - 2. Hishām I (172-180/788-796)
     - 3. Al Ḥakam I (180-207/796-822)
       - 4. ʿAbdul Raḥman II (207-238/822-852)
         - 5. Muḥammad I (238-273/852-886)
           - 6. Al Mundhir (273-275/886-888)
           - 7. ʿAbdullah (275-300/888-912)
             - Muḥammad
               - 8. ʿAbdul Raḥman III (300-350/912-961)
                 - 9. Al Ḥakam II (350-366/961-976)
                   - 10. Hishām II (366-391/976-1000) (401-404/1010-1013)
                 - ʿAbdul Jabbār
                   - Hishām
                     - 11. Muḥammad II (400-401/1009-1010)
                       - 14. ʿAbdul Raḥman V (414-1023)
                 - Sulaymān
                   - Al Ḥakam
                     - 12. Sulaymān (400-401/1009 1010) (404-407/1013-1016)
                 - ʿAbdul Malik
                   - Muḥammad
                     - 13. ʿAbdul Raḥman IV (409-1018)
                     - 16. Hishām III (418-423/1027-1031)
                 - ʿUbaydullah
                   - ʿAbdul Raḥman
                     - 15. Muḥammad III (414-416/1023-1025)

D. *The ῾Abbāsī Dynasty, Al Kūfah* (133–149/750–766) *Baghdād* (149–657/766–1258)

1. THE MAKKAN LINEAGE

Hāshim, Grandfather of the Prophet

῾Abdullah — Abū Ṭālib — Al ῾Abbās, Uncle of the Prophet

Muḥammad, the Prophet — ῾Ali — ῾Abdullah

Al Ḥasan — Al Ḥusayn — ῾Ali

Muḥammad

Al Saffāḥ — Al Manṣūr

2. THE CALIPHS

Al ῾Abbās

1. Abul ῾Abbās Al Saffāḥ (133-137/750-754) — 2. Abu Ja῾far Al Manṣūr (137-159/754-775

3. Al Mahdī (159-169/775-785

4. Al Hādī (169-170/785-786 — 5. Hārūn al Rashīd (170-194/786-809

6. Al Amīn (194-198/809-813 — 7. Al Ma'mūn (198-218/813-833 — 8. Al Mu῾taṣim (218-228/833-842

Muḥammad — 9. Al Wāthiq (228-233/842-847 — 10. Al Mutawakkil (233-247/847-861)

12. Al Musta῾īn (248-252/862-866 — 14. Al Muhtadī (256-257/869-870

11. Al Muntaṣir (247-248/861-862 — 13. Al Mu῾tazz (252-256/866-869 — 15. Al Mu῾tamid (257-279/870-892

16. Al Mu῾taḍid (279-290/892-902

Continued on next page

The Sunnah

17. Al Muqtafī
(290-296/902-908)

18. Al Muqtadir (296-320/908-932)

19. Al Qāhir
(320-323/932-934)

20. Al Raḍī
(323-329/934-940)

21. Al Muttaqī
(329-333/940-944)

23. Al Muṭī[c]
(335-364/946-974)

22. Al Mustakfī
(333-335/944-946)

24. Al Ṭā'i[c]
(364-381/974-991)

25. Al Qadīr
(381-423/991-1031)

26. Al Qā'im
(423-468/1031-1075)

Muḥammad

27. Al Muqtadī
(468-487/1075-1094)

28. Al Mustaẓhir
(487-512/1094-1118)

29. Al Mustarshid
(512-530/1118-1135)

30. Al Rashīd
(530-531/1135-1136)

31. Al Muqtafī
(531-555/1136-1160)

32. Al Mustanjid
(555-566/1160-1170)

33. Al Mustaḍī'
(566-576/1170-1180)

34. Al Nāṣir
(576-622/1180-1225)

35. Al Ẓāhir
(622-623/1225-1226)

36. Al Mustanṣir
(623-640/1226-1242)

37. Al Musta[c]ṣim
(640-656/1242-1258)

Makkans with those of Madīnah. Certainly, his premonition was right and his strategy timely. Both were precious components of his leadership.

Upon arrival in Madīnah in the summer of 622, Muḥammad reconciled the two main tribes of the city and merged them together to form the first Islamic polity. Their alienation and mutual antagonism were traditional. Muḥammad replaced hatred with respect, love, and esteem; estrangement with concern; and division with unity. He then merged the Madīnese (*al Anṣār*) with the Makkans (*al Muhājirūn*) who had come to Madīnah bare-handed and destitute. Every home in Madīnah responded to the appeal by opening its hearth to a Makkan individual or family. It was the first time that chiefs and aristocrats, plebeians and slaves, rich and poor, citizens and aliens merged together to form a new society in which the bond of faith transcended the differences of birth and history; where religious loyalty created for itself an organic socioeconomic, political, and military unity. The union was not restricted to Muslims. Muḥammad persuaded the Jews to join, and they became integral members of the new social order. They too had their differences among themselves, as well as with the Arab and Muslim Madīnese. They were clients of the two dominant tribes, al Aws and al Khazraj, and were involved with the latter in all their disputes and wars. Muḥammad's leadership was strong enough to bring them all under one roof and to weld them together into the first ecumenical, pluralistic society. To formalize their union and record their agreement, Muḥammad dictated the Covenant of Madīnah – the first written constitution in human history. Promulgation of this constitution launched the first Islamic state, the first multireligious world order.[12]

Muḥammad brought all this about with his own wisdom and power of persuasion. Of the power to coerce anyone, he had none. He knew well that a union not fully desired by its members cannot stand, just as the ruler undesired by his people will never succeed. The new society was based on *shūrā* (consultation among peers with a view to achieve consensus, as described in the Qur'ān 42:38) as well as upon a number of principles that have continued to serve as norms of political activity throughout Muslim history. Among others, these principles include the following. Social order is absolutely necessary. "If as few as three of you go out on a mission, you should designate a *khalīfah* (leader), a first successor, and a second successor."[13] This is the old Mesopotamian principle which regards social order as the *conditio sine qua non* of life; the group without a leader is like sheep without a shepherd.[14] The *ummah* is a people with a cause, a mission to be accomplished in space and time, and hence it must be ordered. "Even an unjust *imām,*" Muḥammad said, "is better than chaos or no-order . . . where anybody may take the law into his own hand. . . Naturally, neither case, as such, is felicitous; and yet, an unjust government that maintains order does fulfill an essential good for society." Best of all is the government that fulfills both order and justice. In such a state, obedience to the ruler is a religious and civil duty as long as what is commanded does not contravene the law of God. Where the state departs from the law of God, no obedience is necessary. Because of potential abuse of this condition, Muḥammad carefully warned against it. We should never question the legitimacy of a government's action, he commanded, unless it is obviously *kufran bawāḥan fīhi burhān* (a departure from the law of God confirmed by unquestionable evidence of its occurrence).[15] Within these limitations, every Muslim or citizen is a pastor responsible for his pastorate, the ruler for his state as well as the father for his home, the mother for her children and household, the employee for the interests of his employer.[16] Besides orienting the ship of state toward the goals Islam had prescribed for it, the prime duty of the leadership is to care for the weak, the poor, and all those who need help to fulfill the ultimate and personal goals. "Those leaders who fulfill this function," Muḥammad proclaimed, "earn for themselves a guarantee against the Fire." And history has no regard for those societies that did not care for the weak among them. "Indeed," the Prophet said, "God will provide and give assistance and victory in the measure to which societies show concern for their weak. . . . Whoever shows no mercy to the small among us, and no respect to the great, does not belong to us." Above all, social order should issue in justice for all. To respond to the cry of the victims of injustice – whether Muslim or non-Muslim – is of paramount importance. "Nothing separates that cry from the hearing of God," the Prophet affirmed.

The leadership of the social order must organize its administration so as to maximize its service to the people and minimize the cost. To achieve this objective, competence should be the criterion of employment. "To appoint any leader of any public service, however small, on any other basis," the Prophet declared, "is an act of treason to God, His Prophet and the *ummah.*" The ruler should hold everyone responsible for his deeds and leave the reckoning of intentions to God. But if he starts suspecting people, or pushing them to suspect one another, corruption will spread within that state and bring it to ruin. The ruler should always aim at reconciliation and unity. When a dispute arises between two factions, he should bring them to a just settlement; should any rebel against the settlement, the whole *ummah* should oppose the rebel faction and bring it to its senses.[17] Justice is certainly the first social ideal of Islam. The indignation its violation generates in the Muslim and the enthusiasm for its defense and maintenance know little or no limit in the heart committed to *tawḥīd*. However, like every value, the pursuit of justice can also become oppressive. That is why one should not omit to temper such pursuit with compassion and mercy. This realization, together with his usual sensitivity to the need of the hungry, the weak, and the oppressed, prompted Muḥammad to declare: "When He created humanity, God pledged to Himself that He would always exercise mercy. 'My mercy is stronger than My wrath' – God said." As to his own rule, Muḥammad said: "God did not send me to be a zealot as ruler, nor a fanatic, but an educator and guide to make life easier for humans."

All the foregoing facts of the *sunnah* concretize the values relating to the personal and internal social ethic of Islam. This was an achievement of the Makkan period. The external social ethic of Islam, however, could not come into play until after the Hijrah to Madīnah and the setting up of the *ummah* as a sovereign state. Prior to this event, the *ummah* existed *in potentia*. Even so, it was subject to such persecution that it could not exercise its prerogatives as an *ummah*. Hence, the first concern of the Prophet after the Hijrah, once internal order was established and everybody was assigned to his station, was to turn to the outside world. Obviously the most immediate external problem was the warlike hostility of Makkah, whose leadership had decided to assassinate Muḥammad on the eve of the *Hijrah*. On that night, learning of their plan, the Prophet decided to divert their attention by putting ʿAlī, his cousin, in his bed and covering him with Muḥammad's own green mantle. Muḥammad and Abū Bakr slipped away in the darkness of night. The Makkans forced the door open, pulled the mantle with their swords drawn and found ʿAlī instead of the man they wanted.

Most of the Muslims had by then left Makkah for Madīnah. They left behind them their relatives and properties. The Makkans resorted to harassing the former and confiscating the latter. The Muslim emigrants from Makkah were destitute and had to depend on the hospitality of their hosts. It was natural for them to think of ways of getting back at the Makkans. The caravans of Makkah passed through Madīnah, carrying goods north and south. The Muslims sought to seize what they could, and Makkah mobilized for war. In consequence, the Muslims were dragged into their first military confrontation with their enemies. Three hundred Muslims led by the Prophet met a Makkan army of over one thousand at Badr. Both sides thought that the encounter would be decisive for all time. While the Makkans readied the cream of their men for battle, the Prophet lifted his followers' morale to the highest possible level. He prayed to God aloud, saying, "O God, here is Makkah come to belie Your Prophet and stamp out Your servants. If they win today, You will not be adored in this land. Grant us Your assistance and victory. You alone are our Master, our Help and Succour." Then he turned to the Muslims and said to them that God would answer his prayer and grant them victory; that whoever fell in the coming battle would achieve Paradise and life eternal.[18]

The Prophet's military strategy was questioned by his followers after he declared to them that whereas the cause was divine, the strategy would be human. In consultation with one another, the Muslims decided upon a different deployment of their forces. The battle raged in the afternoon, and losses were heavy on both sides. The Muslims emerged victorious. In fact, it was a miraculous infusion of unusual energy that made the Muslims fight so valiantly as to defeat their enemies despite their preponderous numbers and equipment. However, the Muslims were exhausted and could not press their victory by pursuing the Makkans. They returned to Madīnah satisfied with their victory in a battle, if not in the war. A year later, the Makkans returned for another engagement, which took place outside of Madīnah, at the foot of Mount Uḥud. There, the Muslims lost the battle but inflicted heavy losses upon the Makkans, who could not pursue their victory and occupy Madīnah. Desperate as well as wise from their mistakes, the Makkans launched another last attempt against Muḥammad and his movement. This time they mobilized practically the whole of Arabia and arrived at the gates of Madīnah to destroy the Islamic state, eradicate the Muslims, and finish off their scourge once and for all. With such vastly superior numbers the Muslims could not contend, and they had to stay within their city. In haste, one vulnerable side of the city had to be defended by digging a ditch in front of it, which gave the battle its name.[19] Fortunately for the Muslims, they did not have to fight. A terrible sandstorm swept over the region. It did not affect the Muslims who were inside their own houses and fortresses; but it played havoc with their enemies who were camped in tents over a wide arch on the southern flank of Madīnah right in the path of the storm. The storm uprooted their tents, dispersed and killed most of their mounts, and destroyed their supplies. Those who could managed to run away and the campaign collapsed.

The constitution of the Islamic state (the Covenant of Madīnah) regarded the Jews as an autonomous *ummah* within the state. It endowed the rabbinic court with ultimate authority to adjudicate and settle all Jewish affairs. Since their defeat and dispersion by the Romans, this was the first time that Jewish communal existence and the Torahic law were recognized as legitimate by any state. Nonetheless, the Jews' allegiance to the Islamic state wavered. The Prophet warned them first, then banished some of them, then banished others and confiscated their properties. In the Battle of the Ditch they again played a treacherous role; but it was thwarted only by collapse of the enemy in the sandstorm. This time the Prophet was compelled to execute a number of them and send the rest out of Madīnah. From their exile in Khaybar, their plotting against the Islamic state continued. In time it necessitated a campaign to dislodge and banish them from the Arabian Peninsula altogether. Their fate under Christian Byzantium was no better. However, when the Fertile Crescent was conquered by the forces of Islam, the status under the Covenant of Madīnah was again offered to them without regard to their past relations with the Muslims in the Arabian Peninsula.

Several months after the Battle of the Ditch, on the occasion of the *ḥajj* (pilgrimage), the Prophet decided to perform the pilgrimage ritual with his companions. He invited all the Arab tribes to join him, partly to pay tribute to the Kaʿbah and the Abrahamic tradition which it expressed, and partly to disprove Makkah's claim that the Muslims have no regard for Makkah and its tradition. Upon reaching the outskirts of Makkah, the Makkans came out in force to defend their city against what they thought to be a Muslim invasion. The Prophet had previously declared the religious intention of the trip; but the Makkans did not trust his statement. They feared that once inside the city, the Muslims would take over. Hence, they decreed that there would be no entry for Muslims and no pilgrimage. The occasion called for some negotiation between the two parties, which led to an agreement known as the Treaty of Ḥudaybiyah.

The terms of the covenant spelled humiliation for the Muslims. First, the Muslims were to perform no pilgrimage that year but could return for pilgrimage the following year provided they came devoid of arms and stayed no more than three days. Second, any Makkan who joined them was to be returned to Makkah and any Muslim who defected to Makkah was not to be returned to Madīnah. Third, the Arabs from outside Makkah who wished to join with the city could do so, and those wishing to join with Muḥammad could do so. Fourth, neither side was to attack the other in the next ten years. The Prophet acquiesced in these terms. He calculated that, since Islam was a matter of personal conviction and faith, the Makkan convert to Islam would not apostasize if he were compelled to reside in Makkah; that the presence of the Muslim apostate in Madīnah would be useless and

Jāmiʿ Mosque, Brunei.

even harmful. He also realized that the tribes were autonomous entities. If they wished to join Makkah, no one could stop them by force; but the possibility of persuading them to join the ranks of Islam might prove to be a distinct advantage. As to the ten years of peace, the Prophet took them to be a tremendous gain because peace was exactly what he needed to bring the message of Islam to the whole of Arabia. He equally agreed to postpone the pilgrimage one year in order to have a peaceful pilgrimage at which all Arabs would gather and be informed of the message of Islam firsthand. He was therefore agreeable to signing the treaty. Not so were the senior companions, who regarded the whole treaty as an insult worthy of a violent response. Division and rebellion within Muslim ranks were close at hand. Moreover, the treacherous past of Makkah left no room for Muslim confidence. The Makkans overkept the Muslims' delegate, ʿUthmān ibn ʿAffān, and the rumor spread that they had killed him. What if they took the Muslims by surprise right now and started a battle whose time, place, and conditions were all of their own choosing? How could they be trusted to enter into a covenant of peace?

While the delegates of both camps waited, the Prophet gathered his closest companions under a tree and sat down to reason with them. He asked them to trust in God, in Him and in peace. Equally, he asked them to be ready to fight to the last man should the Makkans cheat. Finally, Muḥammad reasserted his authority as Prophet and reminded them of their covenant to accord him obedience in everything, including laying down their lives. As in all other times of crisis, Abū Bakr was the first to renew his pledge and warned ʿUmar ibn al Khaṭṭāb not to violate his own, which he made when he first entered the ranks of Islam. So ʿUmar renewed his pledge to obey, and the other companions followed, suit. Having restored unity to his camp by this new covenant – later called *Bay*ʿ*at al Riḍwān* or the Covenant of Contentment – the Prophet proceeded to sign the pact with Makkah. The delegates returned safely to their camps, and the Muslims began their journey back to Madīnah.

On the way home, *sūrah* "*Al Fatḥ*" was revealed, opening with the verse: "We have granted you a clear and certain victory; and We have forgiven you all your shortcomings, past and present. We have proffered unto you Our total blessing; and We have guided you onto the straight path."[20] This revelation dissipated whatever doubt remained in the minds of the Muslims concerning the value of the Treaty of Ḥudaybiyah. The following years proved them right.

For the first time, Islam, its Prophet, and its *ummah* as sovereign state were no longer looked upon by the Makkans and their allies as nonentities or runaways from the Quraysh tribe, but as equals with acknowledged title, legitimacy and rights, and a political entity as prominent as Makkah. Second, the pact acknowledged the right of access of Muslims to the Kaᶜbah, and their right to perform the pilgrimage and to worship within the holy sanctuary of Makkah. Third, the peace permitted Muḥammad to send his messengers to the tribes of Arabia without fear for their lives. In two years of Islamic mission in Arabia after the Treaty of Ḥudaybiyah a near majority were converted. When Muḥammad called the Muslims to march on Makkah following Makkah's violation of the Ḥudaybiyah treaty, the numbers that rallied to the call were so preponderant that Makkah was overwhelmed without battle. The peace which Ḥudaybiyah ushered in gave Muḥammad the confidence to send his delegates even outside of Arabia, to Abyssinia, Egypt, Byzantium, Persia, and the tribes on the edges of the Peninsula. Without Ḥudaybiyah, the conquest of Makkah would not have happened so soon, nor would it have been so bloodless.

By instituting peace, the Ḥudaybiyah Treaty allowed the Muslims to present Islam without being regarded as a threat. Since war and hostility were ruled out, the conflict resolved itself into an ideational one presented to reason and conscience, to each individual person as such. Is God God or not? If He is the only Creator, ought He not to be the only Master or Judge? Must not worship and adoration, obedience and service, loyalty and faith be exclusively His? If justice and mercy and temperance are virtues, must they not be God's commandments and hence be obeyed under all circumstances? And if literary eloquence is the noblest and greatest value, is not the Qur'ān so sublime that it must be a revelation from God, a supernatural work by the divine Author? This cool logic of Islam quickly convinced the Arabs of the Peninsula, as it was to convince the millions to whom it was presented later. The ranks of the *ummah* swelled with new recruits every day, and soon Islam became the preponderant voice of most of Arabia.

Abū Baṣīr, a Makkan, converted to Islam and ran away to Madīnah. The people of Makkah asked for his extradition in accordance with the terms of the treaty. Muḥammad called Abū Baṣīr and told him: "We Muslims do not cheat. We pledged to return the runaways, and we must therefore return you to Makkah. Be firm and go back. God will provide for you." Abū Baṣīr surrendered to the Makkan delegates and left. On the way to Makkah, Abū Baṣīr wrestled with his captor, seized his sword, killed him, and ran away. The number of Makkan converts to Islam continued to increase. Since by remaining in Makkah they would expose their lives to danger, they ran away to the desert and lay in wait for Makkan caravan traffic. They disrupted that traffic so badly that Makkah, being unable to contain them, pleaded with the Prophet to alter the terms of the treaty so that the Makkan converts to Islam would fall under Muḥammad's responsibility and he would have to contain them under the terms of the treaty. It was ironic that the term of the treaty that the Muslims found humiliating and objectionable turned out to be advantageous to the Muslims and harmful to Makkah. The Makkans sent Suhayl ibn 'Amr, the delegate who had dictated that ruling, to plead for its repeal.

The next pilgrimage season soon arrived, and Muḥammad called on all Muslims to perform the *ḥajj* with him. Thousands responded and readied themselves to go. Muḥammad taught them how to dress for the pilgrimage, how to perform the ritual, what to say and do. Their procession and entry into Makkah with their *iḥrām* garb, consisting of two white unsown pieces of cloth, their chanting *Labbayka Allahumma Labbayka* (At your call O God, here I come) must have been awe-inspiring to all the Arabs who saw them. It engendered profound respect for them and reverence for their new religion, Islam. The Makkans evacuated their city and positioned themselves on the mountain overlooking the sanctuary. As the Muslims circumambulated the Ka'bah, Muḥammad taught them to chant:

Allahu Akbar, Allahu Akbar, Allahu Akbar
(God is Greater, God is Greater, God is Greater)
Allahu Akbar, Allahu Akbar, Wa Lillahi-l-ḥamd

(God is Greater, God is Greater, to God belongs the praise)
Allahu Akbaru Kabīran, wal ḥamdu lillahi kathīran
(God is Greater, truly Greater; to God belongs all the praise)
Wa subḥāna Allahu bukratan wa aṣīlan
(To God belongs the glory every morning and evening)
Lā ilaha illā Allahu waḥdah
(There is no God but Allah alone)
Ṣadaqa waʿdah, wa aʿazza jundah
(His promise was true; He reinforced with His army)
Wa hazama al aḥzāba waḥdah
(And He alone brought defeat to Makkah and her allies)
Lā ilaha illā Allahu wa la naʿbudu illā iyyāh
(There is no God but Allah. We shall adore none but Him)
Mukhlisīna lahuddīna walaw kariha al mushrikūn
(We shall be candid in our religion to Him, however opposed the associationists may be).

This confession of faith was as candid as it was terrifying and fascinating. Its defiant tone inspired terror in the heart of the enemy without show of arms; and yet it moved those hearts to agree with it by its certain candidness, its firm resolution to adore but one God, its reassurance and optimism that God will give Islam ultimate victory. Equally, the ritual of the *ḥajj* itself confirmed the Muslims' high regard for the Kaʿbah, for Makkah and her Abrahamic tradition. All this made Islam irresistible, at least to two of Makkah's greatest generals, Khālid ibn al Walīd and ʿAmr ibn al ʿĀṣ, who abandoned their fellow Makkans and rushed in front of them to declare their conversion to Islam. Muḥammad received them with open arms and invited them to join in the ceremony.

It was only a few months after this pilgrimage that a tribe allied to Makkah aggressed upon an ally of Madīnah. The Muslims asked the Makkans to fulfill their responsibility under the Ḥudaybiyah Treaty. But the Makkans declined. The Muslims mobilized and called for war. Ten thousand or more horsemen and thousands more on camel back and foot behind them stood at the gates of Makkah within days, ready to lay down their lives at the Prophet's command. Overwhelmed, the

Makkans surrendered. The Prophet entered the city and went straight to the Ka'bah. With his own hands, he struck the idols down, removed the debris from the holy precinct, cleansed and reconsecrated the Ka'bah to the unique God, Master and Creator of all. As he labored he recited: "The truth has become manifest; falsehood is confuted, as it should be."[21] The Makkan leaders stood by, watching and trembling in fear for their lives. Then the Prophet called them to come forth to hear his verdict. They advanced and knelt before him. The Prophet said: "Rise and go forth; you are free," signifying his general pardon to them and to all Makkans. This magnanimity of Muḥammad at his finest hour of triumph dissipated the last resistance in their hearts. First their leaders and then the rank and file came to declare their conversion to Islam. Makkah became a Muslim city; its sanctuary became the holiest shrine of Islam, and its people its foremost defenders.

Finally, the *sunnah* was the concretization of Islam's relevance to international order and relations. The covenant of Madīnah had acknowledged the Jews as an *ummah* and had granted them constitutional autonomy to order their lives as the Torah dictated and as it was interpreted by their own judicial courts and institutions. This constitutional provision did not change when some Jews committed acts of treason against the Islamic state because Islam rejects any theory of vicarious guilt. The acts of treason were the acts of those who committed them, not of their descendants. The same constitutional provision was extrapolated by the Prophet for application to the Christians of Najrān. These had sent a delegation to Madīnah seeking a reassurance regarding their own status and inquiring about Islam. The Christian delegation was met and entertained by the Prophet, who also presented Islam to them. Some of them converted and joined the ranks of the Muslim *ummah*. Those who did not convert were established by the Prophet as another *ummah* within the Islamic state and under its constitution. He sent the delegates back to their people in Yaman guarded from the hazards of the road by Muslims and accompanied by Abū 'Ubaydah, whom he appointed as state representative in their midst.

The Islamic state, therefore, was by the Prophet's own design and implementation a multireligious order which brought together under the order of peace and legitimacy Muslims, Jews, and Christians. This pluralism was not a matter of courtesy but was constitutional; not a matter of tolerating the alien customs of food, dress, or music, but the whole corpus of laws that governed the life of the non-Muslim religious community. The pluralism of the Islamic state was a pluralism of laws, an innovation unheard of elsewhere in the history of mankind. The Islamic state of Madīnah was a microcosm of the world order to be. The act of bringing the Christians of Najrān under the Constitution was to be repeated by his companions in favor of the Zoroastrian Persians, and by their successors in favor of the Hindus and Buddhists, and of all other religions.

Following the peace with Makkah, Muḥammad had sent delegations to the kings around Arabia inviting them to join Islam. If they did not accept to convert, after hearing the presentation of the delegates, they were invited to join the *Pax Islamica,* the international order of peace under which ideas are free to move and humans are free to convince and be convinced of the truth while preserving their political, economic, social, cultural, even military establishments intact. The Islamic state sought an opportunity to present Islam to all humans everywhere and would honor their personal decisions to accept or reject it. It was not interested in subjugating them, nor in exploiting them in any way. It sought not its own interest but their own as equal human beings, as creatures of God like themselves, entitled to have the revelation conveyed to them. The Islamic state's mission was restricted to conveying that message from God. The decision to accept or reject it was to be entirely man's, just as God had said (Qur'ān 18:29). But no power, institution, or tradition may prevent humans from hearing and considering the divine call. That would be to assume their incapacity to judge for themselves, which, besides being both false and insulting, is a kind of spiritual tyranny over them.

This is why the Prophet's delegates were instructed to tell the kings and chieftains that every ruler must bear responsibility for the spiritual welfare of his subjects. The emperor of Byzantium, the ruler of Egypt, and the Negus of Abyssinia responded with kind words. The emperor of Persia and the chieftains of the buffer states in Northern Arabia rejected the call with contempt and defiance. The ruler of Dhāt al Ṭalḥ, a vassal of Byzantium, killed all fifteen of the Prophet's companions who were sent to present Islam to him and his people. The governor of Buṣrā, another agent of Byzantium, killed the Muslim delegate upon hearing him deliver his message. Some Muslim historians have reported that Emperor Heraclius himself gave the order to the provincial governors to mobilize and engage in hostilities.[22] This response from Byzantium and its satellites prompted the Muslims to seek to break the authority obstructing the promulgation of the divine message. The options of these defiant rulers were further restricted by their foolhardy actions. The Muslim armies gathering at their door offered them three possibilities: to accept Islam; to accept the world order of Islam in which they would exist as a constituent *ummah,* free to exercise their religion and guaranteed their human and corporate rights; or war. As for the Muslims themselves, their spirit was typified by ʿAbdullah ibn Rawāḥah, a companion of the Prophet in command of the army at Maʿān, southeast of the Dead Sea. Before engaging the enemy, he told his men: "Brothers! That which some people fear might happen to us is precisely the reason why we came here; namely, martyrdom. We Muslims fight neither with numbers nor equipment. Our only power is in our faith, which God has graciously granted to us. Rise to battle and march forward! One of the two greatest blessings shall be ours: either victory or martyrdom. In either case we are the winners." A similar spirit moved the Muslims confronting the Persian Empire. The Persian supreme commander, in an attire so resplendent and covered with gold that he could hardly move, sent after the Muslim commander who was clad in the usual desert attire. "What brings you here to fight us?," the Persian asked. The Muslim commander answered: "That humans may stop worshipping humans and offer worship to the Creator of humans. To fulfill this end, our men are as eager to die as your men are eager to live."

In the tenth year of the *Hijrah* (632 C.E.) the Prophet led a procession of over 100,000 Muslims from Madīnah to Makkah to perform the *Ḥajj.* These thousands had come from all corners of the Peninsula to accompany the Prophet on his pilgrimage. Thousands more joined the procession en route, and others went directly to Makkah. On this occasion, the Prophet delivered the sermon that was to be his last. In it he summed up the message of which he was the divinely appointed trustee.

Mounted on his camel and with Rabīʿah ibn Umayyah by his side on another camel to repeat his words so that everyone would hear, the Prophet said:

> O Men, listen well to my words, for I do not know whether I shall meet you again on a like occasion. Until you meet your Lord, the safety of lives and of your property shall be as inviolate as this holy day and holy month. . . . You will indeed meet your Lord and He will reckon your deeds. Whoever is keeping anything that does not belong to him must return it to its rightful owner. . . . All interest is abolished; and all interest due shall be waived; only your capital is yours. . . . You will neither inflict, nor suffer any injustice or iniquity. . . . God has commanded that all interest due to ʿAbbās ibn ʿAbd al Muṭṭalib and his clan [to which Muḥammad was heir] in pre-Islamic days shall be waived. . . . O Men, Satan has lost hope of ever being worshipped in your land. Nevertheless, he is still capable of determining the lesser of your deeds. . . . O men, to you a right belongs with respect to your women, and to your women a right with respect to you, plus kindness. . . . Do treat them well and be kind to them, for they are your partners and committed helpers. . . . I am leaving with you the Book of God and the *sunnah* of His Prophet. If you follow them, you will never go astray.[23]

Eighty-one days after he delivered this sermon, the Prophet died. He had been ill for ten days, and he suffered from a strong fever. Before he was buried, his companions gathered to ponder their fate after his departure. His death was a terrible shock which caused some of them to lose their common sense. In their grief, they were responsive to the plea of ʿUmar, which he voiced at that meeting, that Muḥammad had not died, that God had lifted him up to Heaven as He did Jesus before, and that he continued to live. Abū Bakr arrived late to that meeting. Overhearing ʿUmar, Abū Bakr nudged him to sit down and keep quiet. But ʿUmar persisted, and spoke even louder. Abū Bakr rose and addressed the assembled Muslims: "O People, if you have been worshipping Muḥammad, then know that Muḥammad is dead, dead, dead. But if you have been worshipping God, then know that God is eternal and never dies. God said in His Holy Book: 'Muḥammad is but

Ince Minare Madrasah, Konya, Turkey, 1260-1265.

a human messenger like other messengers before him. If he died or were killed, would you then forsake your faith [that only God is God?]'" (Qur'ān 3:144). That was the last time the Muslim world heard of any attempt to deify Muḥammad, or to ascribe to him any of the supernatural qualities that belong exclusively to God.

Before that occasion, on the death of his son Ibrahīm, born to him of his Egyptian wife Maryam, Muḥammad was struck with overwhelming grief. Since he had no male progeny, the birth of Ibrahīm had meant a great hope for him, which he expressed by choosing the ancestral name for the child. His premature death as an infant of only a few months depressed Muḥammad severely. At that moment, some companion suggested that the baby did not die, but was taken by God and lived with Him. Looking at the dead infant he held in his arms, Muḥammad said: "O Ibrahīm, the fact that you are the son of Muḥammad, the Prophet of God, is of no avail to you whatever, as you meet your Creator. The sun and the moon are signs of God. They neither shine nor set for anyone; nor are they eclipsed for the death of anyone. Nothing avails a human except his deeds."

NOTES

1. Qur'ān 3:32, 132; 4:58, 79.
2. Qur'ān 4:58; 33:36; 8:1.
3. Qur'ān 5:3.
4. Qur'ān 5:67; 4:79
5. Qur'ān 42:48; 10:99.
6. Qur'ān 2:142; 10:25; 6:88; 22:16; 24:35.
7. Qur'ān 80:1–10.
8. Qur'ān 16:125; 41:34.
9. Ibn Isḥaq, *Sīrat,* Vol. I, pp. 223–224.
10. Ibn Isḥaq, *Sīrat Rasul Allah*. Translated by Guillaume, A., *The Life of Muhammad* (Oxford: Oxford University Press, 1955), pp. 151–2.
11. Muḥammad Ḥusayn Haykal, *The Life of Muḥammad,* trans. I. R. al Fārūqī (Indianapolis: American Trust Publications, 1396/1976), Chap. 26, pp. 429–442.
12. Ibn Isḥaq, *Sīrat,* Vol. II, pp. 348–357; Haykal, *The Life of Muḥammad,* pp. 180–183.
13. Narrated on behalf of ʿAbdullah ibn ʿAmr ibn al ʿĀṣ by Aḥmad ibn Ḥanbal in *Al Musnad* (Cairo: Dār al Maʿārif, n.d.), Vol. 2, p. 176. The same *ḥadīth* was reported by Abū Dawūd in *Al Sunan.*
14. Thorkild Jacobsen, "Mesopotamia: The Good Life," in H. Frankfort (ed.), *Before Philosophy* (Baltimore: Penguin Books, 1964), p. 217.
15. As reported by al Bukhārī, Muslim, and Aḥmad ibn Ḥanbal.
16. This *ḥadīth* was reported by Muslim.
17. Qur'ān 49:9.
18. Ibn Isḥaq, *Sīrat,* Vol. 2, p. 457; Haykal, *The Life of Muḥammad,* pp. 226–227.
19. Ibn Isḥaq, *Sīrat,* Vol. 3, pp. 699ff; Haykal, *The Life of Muḥammad,* pp. 299ff.
20. Qur'ān 48:1ff.
21. Qur'ān 17:81.
22. Haykal, *The Life of Muḥammad,* pp. 338–389.
23. Ibn Isḥaq, *Sīrat,* Vol. 4, pp. 1022ff.; Haykal, *The Life of Muḥammad,* pp. 486–488.